THE PEER TUTORING HANDBOOK

Promoting Co-operative Learning

Keith Topping

CROOM HELM
London & Sydney

BROOKLINE BOOKS
Cambridge, Massachusetts

© 1988 Keith Topping
Croom Helm Ltd, Provident House,
Burrell Row, Beckenham, Kent BR3 1AT

Croom Helm Australia, 44-50 Waterloo Road,
North Ryde, 2113, New South Wales

British Library Cataloguing in Publication Data

Topping, Keith
  The peer tutoring handbook: promoting
  co-operative learning.
  1. Peer-group tutoring of students
  I. Title
  371.3   LC41

  ISBN 0-7099-4348-2
  ISBN 0-7099-4353-9 Pbk

Brookline Books, PO Box 1046,
Cambridge, MA. 02238

Library of Congress Cataloging-in-Publication Data

Topping, Keith J.
  The peer tutoring handbook.

  Bibliography: p.
  Includes index.
  1. Peer-group tutoring of students. I. Title.
LC41.T67   1987   371.3'94   87-21805
ISBN 0-914797-42-5
ISBN 0-914797-43-3 (pbk.)

**Printed and bound in Great Britain
by Billing & Sons Limited, Worcester.**

Contents

Make your friends your teachers
and mingle the pleasures of conversation
with the advantages of instruction.

Baltasar Gracian (1647)

1

Introduction

Of course, we've been doing it for years. Children have always helped other children, whether encouraged to or not. In the early years of schooling there is an enormous amount of co-operative play in sand, water and other materials. Through the primary school, children work together on language and reading games, on the computer and later in small groups on 'topics' of particular interest. So what's new?

In the past, many schools have had informal arrangements whereby children help other children of the same or lesser age. In many cases, these arose spontaneously. The term 'peer tutoring' implies a system more developed and better articulated than these *ad hoc* and often rather random events. Inherent in the concept of peer tutoring are careful organisation and definite purpose. 'Structure' is evident — although by no means a rigid and inhibiting form of this. Tutoring is usually characterised by careful matching of tutor and tutee, specification of frequent and regular contact times, training in some form of tutoring technique including correction procedures, clear specification of curriculum content and possibly materials, a system for monitoring and supervision, and possibly some form of evaluation.

Suddenly, it all begins to sound a bit alarming. Merely giving it the label of 'peer tutoring' seems to set it apart from everyday practice, and imparts a faintly academic and scientific air to the whole procedure. Now you're less sure that you already know what it's all about. And that makes you feel a tiny bit nervous. The old 'warm fuzzy' has become a 'cold prickly' (Davies and Layton 1974).

For those who work in high schools, the sense of *déja vu* is likely to be less strong. Educational establishments for adolescent pupils usually feature styles of teaching and learning which are less interactive and more didactic than those considered appropriate to younger children. The co-operation which characterises 7-year-olds in the elementary school has often largely disappeared by the time these children have doubled their age, as co-operation increasingly comes to be construed as 'cheating'. How often we complain about the egocentrism of adolescents, without considering how adults have made them that way.

CO-OPERATION VERSUS COMPETITION

Is the schooling process a competition in absorbing prescribed knowledge from the teacher? Or is it a collaborative group experience in which children learn much from each other for their own needs and purposes?

A system which fosters competition implies laurels for the winners — and inevitably dooms the majority to failure. It has been proposed that there are three main ways in which the instructional process may be structured: co-operatively, competitively and individualistically. In a co-operative structure, as one pupil achieves, others automatically achieve also. In a competitive structure, when one achieves, the others automatically *do not* achieve. In an individualistic structure, pupils' goals are unrelated and independent, and when one pupil achieves his or her goal, other students are unaffected, and probably largely indifferent.

Co-operative learning has been the subject of considerable recent study (e.g. Sharan 1980). Johnson and Johnson (1983) made an experimental comparison of the effects of co-operative, competitive and individualistic learning experiences on handicapped and non-handicapped pupils. The results indicated that co-operative learning experiences, as compared with competitive or individualistic ones, promoted more interpersonal attraction between handicapped and non-handicapped pupils, and promoted higher self-esteem and greater empathy on the part of all the children. Co-operative learning promoted greater verbal interaction and physical closeness. At the end of the experience, the handicapped children still had lower self-esteem on average than the non-handicapped children, but this was much less so for those who had been members of the 'co-operative' group. The authors note that all too frequently where handicapped children are integrated into mainstream education, they are expected to survive in the context of a competitive or individualistic system.

THE SOCIAL EFFECTS OF TUTORING

Peer tutoring is 'humanly rewarding' (Goodlad 1979). The tutors learn to be nurturant towards their tutees. They develop a sense of pride and accomplishment, and learn trust and responsibility. Many teachers operating peer tutor projects find the most striking effect is the increased confidence and sense of adequacy in the *tutors*.

This is not to be wondered at. Fowler *et al.* (1986) document the therapeutic effect achieved with disruptive boys by appointing them to check on the behaviour of their classmates during free play periods — 'appointment to the role of peer monitor may itself function as an intervention'. Tutors demonstrate or 'model' correct responses for the tutees to imitate, so the peer tutoring process automatically incorporates constant flattering of the sincerest kind for the 'senior partner' of the pair. It is always fascinating to see for how many children the peer tutoring session is the favourite part of the school day. If the procedure were not popular with the children themselves, and relied purely on teacher direction for its existence, it could not be sustained beyond a few weeks.

Allen (1976) has commented that we live in an 'ageist' society, wherein values and norms are associated increasingly with membership in a broad age category. Little contact occurs between persons fairly close in age, and even less between those disparate in age unless they are members of the same family. Children spend by far the greater proportion of their time with same-age peers — during school time and out of school as well. It has been noted that 12-year-old children spent twice as much time with their age peers as they did with their own parents. At school, the playground may be segregated by age and status, whether officially or unofficially.

Cross-age peer tutoring should prove an excellent mechanism for facilitating social interchange and growth between members of a school which is only in a nominal sense a community. From the tutee's point of view, being a 'friend' of a high-status older child is likely to enhance the youngster's self-esteem. Children are extremely important to children, and this may be particularly true as they approach and enter adolescence, and retreat from the influence of parents. The peer tutorial relationship has few of the institutional and authoritarian over-tones of relationships between professional teachers and children. There is no need to maintain a distance, and genuine affection characterises the interaction between many pairs, in contrast to the production line bonhomie of the professional. Interestingly, Goodlad (1979) proposes that via such projects tutors may gain insights into the processes and difficulties of teaching, which may bring them to greater responsiveness to their own professional adult teachers.

There are a number of research studies which have deliberately used peer tutoring of sorts primarily for the social gains which can accrue from it. Participants in such projects have included language delayed pre-schoolers, socially isolated 5-year-olds, previously ostracised mentally handicapped mainstream children, and pupils in primary and high schools manifesting emotional and behavioural problems. These studies will be reviewed in detail later.

THE INTELLECTUAL EFFECTS OF TUTORING

A more satisfactory social life is all very well, but friends come and friends go, especially when you're a child — so what endures? The research evidence is incontrovertible on this. Peer tutoring improves the attainment in the tutored subject area of both *tutor* and *tutee*. Although the tutors may be covering again material they had been presumed to have mastered, there are nevertheless gains from this process. The tutors may be reviewing and consolidating existing knowledge, filling in gaps, finding extra meanings, and reformulating their knowledge into new conceptual frameworks. Above all, they are likely to remember the material better from experience of the need to put knowledge to some purpose. Many centuries ago Comenius commented: '*Qui docet, discit*' ('Who teaches, learns'). More recently, Briggs (1975) has re-expressed this: 'To teach is to learn twice'.

The benefits for the tutee are considerable. Given one-to-one attention individualisation of learning is possible. Tasks can be selected to suit ideally the sole recipient of the tutoring and the speed of presentation constantly adjusted for optimum learning. There is the opportunity for *demonstration* of the required behaviour, a pleasant change from the verbal harangue which is often all the harassed teacher can find time for. The tutee receives regular and responsive feedback on the correctness of his or her efforts, and is subject to close monitoring which maximises the amount of time spent on-task. Verbal and other social reinforcement is readily available, and of a particularly personal and powerful kind if the relationship is working well. The quality of teaching provided by tutors may not quite match that of professional teachers, but there is a great deal more of it, suffused with the rosy glow of companionship.

THE SCOPE OF PEER TUTORING

The variety of programmes which have operated successfully is prodigious. They range from the relatively structured to the relatively unstructured, from those which emphasise personal and social growth to those which lay great stress on academic achievement, from small supplementary programmes co-ordinated by one teacher to extensive schemes which involve all the pupils in a school, from those which provide help for handicapped pupils of low attainment to those which were designed as enrichment for the relatively able, and from those which focus on the very young to those which concern themselves with the distinctly elderly.

In this latter respect, some successful projects have included 5-year-old tutees, and some *tutors* of the same age or younger, although the latter is rarer. At the other end of the age spectrum, Fletcher and Fawcett (1978) describe an open learning centre for low-income adults which operates on a peer tutor basis, and many other programmes in this field have utilised adult peer volunteers.

Children have been deployed as agents of change in ways other than occupying the role of 'teacher'. There is a great number of research studies reporting the utilisation of classroom peers to improve problematic behaviour of target children within the school (e.g. Strain 1981). Children have effectively offered therapeutic 'counselling' to other children (Warner and Scott 1974), and the evidence suggests that this is no less effective than counselling offered by professional adults (Topping 1983). There is evidence that counselling by adults can, of itself, improve the reading attainment of pupils with learning difficulties (e.g. Lawrence 1972). This approach was developed further by Murfitt and Thomas (1983), who deployed members of the peer group as counsellors to raise the self-concept and reading attainment of high school aged slow learning pupils.

Peer tutoring is extending to increasingly esoteric subject areas. Thus, Fitz-Gibbon and Reay (1982) have used the method widely in foreign language teaching, while Karegianes *et al.* (1980) report on the effects of 'peer editing' on the writing proficiency of low achieving high school students. Cicirelli (1976) extensively explored the use of siblings as tutors of younger children in their own family. Peer tutoring has also been extended to less probable populations, including projects which have operated with young male offenders in youth custody facilities (Posen 1983). Finally, some programmes are beginning to break down the distinction between tutor and tutee, with the implicit ability differential, and are exploring 'reciprocal' or role

5

reversal peer tutoring (e.g. Pigott *et al.* 1986; Palincsar and Brown 1986).

THE TWO-SIGMA PROBLEM

Benjamin Bloom and his students and colleagues at the University of Chicago have been searching for some years for a solution to what they call the 'two-sigma problem'.

Sigma is the symbol for standard deviation, which as many readers will know is a statistical entity which indicates the range of variability in any set of data, such as pupils' scores on attainment tests. Under normal circumstances, from the exact average score, two standard deviations above the mean encompasses all but the top 2.3 per cent of children, and two standard deviations below the mean encompasses all but the bottom 2.3 per cent.

A series of studies were undertaken to compare differences in final achievement measures for groups of children taught under various educational systems. In relation to the standard deviation (sigma) of the control group class, which was taught under conventional conditions, it was found that the *average* student exposed to one-to-one tutoring was about two standard deviations above the average of the control group class. In other words, the average tutored pupil outperformed 98 per cent of the pupils in the control group class.

Bloom's tutoring studies included many where adults served as tutors rather than peers. The 'two-sigma problem' was to find other educational systems which could begin to approach the effectiveness of tutoring while operating in larger groups. Although certain forms of 'mastery learning' were beginning to approach the effectiveness of tutoring, and in combination with other special measures had produced effect sizes as large as 1.7 sigma, tutoring remained the only intervention to have broken the two-sigma barrier. About 90 per cent of tutored students and 70 per cent of mastery learning students attained a level of achievement reached by only the highest 20 per cent of students under conventional instructional conditions.

Bloom comments that: 'The tutoring process demonstrates that *most of the students* do have the potential to reach this high level of learning.' He points out that one-to-one tutoring by adults is too costly for most societies to bear on a large scale. Although peer tutoring is associated with lower effect sizes than adult tutoring, in tandem with other educational components of proven effectiveness, it should prove a powerful tool indeed.

THE MOTHER OF INNOVATION

Peer tutoring originally arose because of stark economic necessity. There were not enough teachers to go round. By serendipity, the system was found to have virtues and qualities which professional teachers could not replicate, and has thus become popular in modern times when teachers are plentiful.

But *are* teachers plentiful? In pursuit of the two-sigma effect, there is clearly still a thread of economic exigency. However numerous today, teachers are an expensive resource, and high cost carries an implication of scarcity.

Goodlad (1979) notes that school teaching is labour-intensive and presents no direct economic benefits. It is thus easy for the education system to be perceived as a burden, particularly in times of recession. Education departments are typically by far the largest spenders in local government facilities. In any case, recession or no, professional teachers cannot do it all. The process of education is too enormous to be driven by a corps of paid professionals alone. Much the same argument has been posited by Albee (1968) with respect to the field of mental health. The role of the professionals is increasingly one of resource management and less one of direct service, in the search for ever increasing overall effectiveness.

CONTEXTS FOR INDEPENDENT LEARNING

This search for ever increasing effectiveness, for expanded influence for professional teachers, can however lead us onto some dangerous ground. In the United States, there has been great emphasis in peer tutoring projects on detailed monitoring, highly structured materials, group and individual contingencies for success, and payment for tutors. The intention seems to be to make the peer tutor a (pale) shadow of the professional adult teacher. Too many of the North American projects seem to be wanting to turn children into mini-teachers.

The European flavour of peer tutoring is rather different. It emphasises clarity of purpose and careful organisation, but prefers simpler tutoring techniques which can be operated effectively within the existing social nexus of the community and within existing resources. The assumption is that a project of this sort is much more likely to endure and spread to other curriculum areas and other children — and other schools. Attention must be paid to those qualities of the peer tutoring interaction which are fundamentally different

7

from other forms of teaching, and therefore perhaps complementary to the latter. We should not set out to make peer tutors more like professional teachers — perhaps it would make more sense to encourage professional teachers to be more like peer tutors.

It may be instructive to take a brief look at a nation where cross-age interaction is encouraged in a way which permeates the fabric of everyday life. Bronfenbrenner (1970) noted that in the Soviet Union there is much involvement by adults and older children in the social life of youngsters; Soviet children are explicitly taught in school to help each other, and especially to help younger children. Classes of older pupils often 'adopt' a younger class, and older children help younger children with school work and by reading stories to them. The adoption system is extended to the world of grown-ups — a factory, shop or office takes responsibility for a class of school children.

Peer tutoring should occur in a context of wider social responsiveness. Glynn (1985) argues that it is within responsive social contexts that individuals acquire not only specific skills but all generic knowledge about *how* to learn. He asserts: 'It is this generic knowledge that allows individuals a measure of control over, and hence independence in, these social contexts.'

The education system is ever more replete with core curricula and carefully detailed aims and objectives, some of which are to do with social skills and achieving individual autonomy and independence as a learner. Yet there is a sense that the harder these things are taught, the less they are learnt, because the way of teaching them does not enshrine the methodology which the teaching is intended to impart.

Glynn argues that in many classrooms at all levels of education, individual learners have minimal control over learning interactions and hence are excessively dependent on external control by teachers. He continues to specify four major characteristics of environments conducive to responsive and independent learning. The first is that the learner must be able to *initiate* rather than merely react to stimuli controlled by another. The second characteristic is the sharing of activity between less skilled and more skilled performers, between whom there is a positive social relationship. This implies that the particular learning task be functional for both performers. The third characteristic is that of reciprocity or mutual influence, with each participant in the interaction modifying the behaviour of the other. The fourth characteristic of the responsive learning context relates to the amount and type of feedback provided for the initiation of the learners.

Teachers criticise more than they praise, although the balance of research evidence overwhelmingly suggests that attending to *required* behaviour produces more effective learning. Feedback procedures should be devised which are democratic in nature, and allow learners to take increasing control of their own growth and development. Glynn argues that by handing over greater control to the learner, teachers would be providing for strong generalisation of what is learned into new contexts, and particularly into contexts where the learner must perform independently of teacher support or control.

PROFESSIONAL PAY-OFFS

We have dealt at length, perhaps excessively, on the benefits of peer tutoring for the tutors and tutees. So what do *teachers* get out of it? Goodlad (1979) notes that peer tutoring programmes can free teachers from much routine work, leaving them to carry out more technical and truly professional tasks. Monitoring tutor programmes is, by definition, inherently more personal than monitoring a whole class, and tends to be more rewarding as well as relieving the strain of monitoring all the members of a large group simultaneously.

For one teacher with a class of 30 pupils to serve as an efficient and effective direct educator is frankly impossible, as any teacher who has desperately tried to hear every member of a primary school class reading every day will readily agree. All too often this ends up with one child reading to the teacher, while another dozen wait at the teacher's desk for attention in respect of other problems; administrative interruptions and problems with deviant behaviour compound the awfulness of the situation. Omniscience is not a contractual requirement. Teachers must increasingly function as managers of effective learning, rather than the font of all available wisdom.

Doyle and Lobl (1987) note that there can be considerable practical *dis*advantages in peer tutoring. It may be difficult to provide sufficient comfort and intimacy for large numbers of children, and noise levels may prove distracting for other pupils. With young children or those of limited ability, the quality of tutoring may leave a good deal to be desired. Tutors may be able to conform to a simple structure, but lack the skills to elicit initiation from their tutees. Some tutors may too readily assume an over-dominant and authoritarian role with their tutee (one wonders where this kind of teaching relationship has been modelled). Unless the tutoring technique, materials and process are fine tuned by supervising professionals, some tutors may become

9

rather bored. Some relationships in tutoring pairs may prove problematic. If tutoring is to occur during school hours, interference with other curriculum activities may prove irritating to some teachers. Parents may misunderstand the purpose and methods of the project, and complain in a vociferous if uninformed way.

On the other hand, the advantages are many. Children usually acquire the tutoring procedures a great deal more quickly than teachers anticipate. Characteristically, they show considerable self-discipline during the tutoring process, which may be an indication that they find it self-reinforcing. The interaction between a vast majority of pairs is usually manifestly positive, and good relationships endure beyond the tutoring situation. Because the peer tutor project is 'special' its integral subject material enjoys high status during and after the project.

Peer tutoring is easy to set up because the pairs are always on hand. It is easy to monitor the technique being used by the tutors, and to correct any faults or problems. Using existing materials in schools, the project incurs no extra expenditure of money, and relatively little in terms of additional teacher time. The regularity of tutoring sessions can be ensured. If necessary, tutoring partners can be changed round without undue ruffling of feathers. Social skills and positive attitudes are developed in both tutors and tutees, in addition to the gains in attainment accruing to both members of the pair. The latter is undoubtedly the main attraction for teachers in peer tutoring projects — they 'kill two birds with one stone', since both tutors and tutees improve their skills (with very few exceptions). Very few of these latter advantages are true of projects which involve parents in tutoring their children at home, although these have other advantages of a different sort.

GREAT EXPECTATIONS

A large volume of encouragement may be necessary to stir the faint-hearted teacher into action, but beware of expecting too much. Nothing is achieved without effort, and 'he that would have the fruit must climb the tree', as Fuller wrote in 1732. Although peer tutoring is highly cost-effective, as with all else in life, there *is* a cost. The good news is that, as also with other things in life, it gets easier with practise. This does however have the implication that your first project *must* work, and be seen to work, and therefore a great deal of extra effort must be expended on your first venture. You need success for yourself, and for the credibility of the approach among the kids in the playground, among the teachers in the staff room, and among the parents at the school gate.

All of this implies that you should start small, with careful attention to detail. Goodlad (1979) notes that many ambitious peer tutoring schemes have been fraught with timetabling and organisation problems, and have expired as the steam ran out. Thus it is advocated that you start with peer tutoring within one school, and preferably within one class. This of course is very like the original concept of the tutorial community. True age-peer tutoring within an already existing social group is the easiest to organise. If you succeed with this, extend to cross-age peer tutoring involving children from another class. If you succeed with this, experiment with bringing in tutors from another school or from a college. But if you get to this point, do not expect university teachers to show any great understanding of the educative process, since their own institutions are light years behind the schools in pedagogic methodology. College students may be more successfully deployed as 'peer' tutors during the long holiday on a 'summer school' basis. Likewise, start out with a straightforward curriculum area amenable to the approach, and a straightforward and self-reinforcing technique for the tutoring pairs. As your competence increases, extension to more exotic curricular areas can be attempted. Beyond this, the tutoring of adults by adults on an age-peer basis is perfectly possible, although difficult to organise and sustain. There is no end to the possibilities of the peer tutoring format for the imaginative teacher.

What follows will inform you about the history of tutoring, research on its effectiveness, and the operation of some seminal projects. Perhaps more crucially, for those in the early stages of 'kayak angst', it will provide detailed information on planning, organising, running and evaluating a project. Throughout, the emphasis will be on ensuring that the first simple small-scale project succeeds. After that, you will have learnt far more from experience than you could ever learn from reading here. However, it will always be worthwhile to return to this book to review what you are doing. Otherwise, you may repeat one experience many times subsequently, and fail to derive *all* the potential benefits peer tutoring offers.

2

The History of Tutoring

Many teachers, official and unofficial, are likely to have used tutoring in some shape or form. Arrangements which have some of the features of present day tutoring have been reported from ancient Rome and in the early practices of Judaism. Allen (1976) documents the contention that the idea of childhood as a separate category of life did not exist prior to the sixteenth or seventeeth centuries. Thus, once past the age of 5 or 7 years, the child became part of the world of adults, acquiring work and social skills by participation through modelling in an informal apprenticeship system.

It was only toward the end of the Middle Ages in England that some teachers began to group together those pupils studying the same curriculum area. Subsequently, 'classes' became established on the same basis, still relating to homogeneity of curriculum tasks. It was not until considerably later, towards the middle of the eighteenth century, that the grouping of pupils with reference to their chronological age became at all a common practice. So the whole social structure of schooling facilities was very different, and it is difficult to know whether this would have facilitated or inhibited the development of tutoring arrangements. Certainly during all this period the core curriculum was very narrow and rigid, methods of teaching were preoccupied with rote learning, and classes were extremely large, but it is only this latter feature which is likely to have directly promoted the development of tutoring. Nevertheless, we do know that 'monitors' were employed in Elizabethan grammar schools during the latter half of the sixteenth century.

THE INNOVATIONS OF ANDREW BELL

However, the first *systematic* use of peer tutoring in the world is undoubtedly associated with the name of Andrew Bell, who was born on 27 March 1753. In 1789, Bell was appointed superintendent of a charity school for the orphaned sons of soldiers at Madras. Bell found the school's teachers resistant to some of the new educational ideas he wished to introduce, and so he turned to experimenting with monitors or peer tutors using these new ideas. He rapidly became aware that the use of children to teach other children was an innovation of greater significance than the new ideas themselves.

Bell's system was astonishingly systematic, and certainly far ahead of its time. Each class was paired into tutors and tutees and to each class was attached an 'assistant teacher' to supervise and instruct the tutors. The assistant teacher reported to a teacher, who reported to 'ushers' who in turn reported to the 'school master'. Every member of the school community had a specified role and clearly defined tasks.

Bell's school incorporated classes in which pupils were grouped according to achievement rather than chronological age, and pupils were promoted or demoted in a way akin to the workings of the current 'grade' system in North America. Bell found the motivation of his pupils much improved, and in his account of the school (published in October 1797) reported 'for months together it has not been found necessary to inflict a single punishment'. Bell remarked:

> The very moment you nominate a boy a tutor, you have exalted him in his own eyes, and given him a character to support, the effect of which is well known. The tutors enable their pupils to keep pace with their classes. Another advantage is that the tutor far more effectually learns his lesson than if he had not to teach it to another. By teaching he is best taught. Still another advantage is that there is a grand stimulus to emulation; for what disgrace attaches to the boy who by his negligence is degraded into a pupil, and falls perhaps to be tutored by his late pupil, promoted to be a tutor!

Virtually all the positions in Bell's elaborate hierarchy were filled by the pupils, ranging in age from 7 to 14 years. This complex arrangement was likened by Bell to the organisation of the army, and he saw the introduction of 'monitors' as akin to the deployment of non-commissioned officers.

The effects of this system in raising pupil attainment appeared to be substantial. Thus Bell reported:

> Firsken, of 12 years and 8 months, with his assistants of 7, 8, 9 and 11 years of age, has taught boys of 4, 5 and 6 years to read *The Spectator* distinctly, and spell every word accurately as they go along, who were only initiated into the mysteries of their A, B, C eight months before.

Bell saw his design for peer tutoring as an efficient system — 'like the steam engine or spinning machinery it diminishes labour and multiplies work . . . ' However, Bell equally emphasised the moral and psychological benefits of his scheme, claiming also that it 'cultivates the best dispositions of the heart by teaching children to take an early and well-directed interest in the welfare of one another'.

THE 'IMPROVEMENTS' OF JOSEPH LANCASTER

Born 25 November 1778, Joseph Lancaster was to open his first school just 20 years later. The school was intended to provide education for disadvantaged children who would not otherwise obtain it. In 1801 Lancaster opened the Borough Road School for 350 boys in London. He arranged classes on the basis of attainment, and deployed monitors and assistant monitors to each class to ensure that the pupils helped each other. Less use was made of consistent tutorial 'pairs' than was the case in the Bell system.

Lancaster was an enthusiastic proponent of the use of carefully structured curriculum materials. He felt that this maximised efficient learning on the part of the tutees, and made the monitors considerably more effective. It also ensured that no pupil sat idle while waiting for further work. Subsequently Lancaster refined his organisation so that pupils were grouped according to the *individual* curriculum areas — i.e. were placed in 'sets'. Using highly structured materials, there was less need for a substantial differential in achievement between tutor and tutee in the curriculum task to be mastered.

Lancaster was a vigorous publicist for the new methods, and Bell reported in 1817 that in England and Wales about 100,000 children were being taught by the 'Bell-Lancaster' system. (It would be more accurate to say the Bell system or the Lancaster system. Essentially, Bell was the innovator and Lancaster the developer and disseminator.) Lancaster's own report on his work appeared in 1803.

THE DECLINE OF THE BELL-LANCASTER SYSTEM

Andrew Bell returned to England from India at around the turn of the century, and in 1804 when he had a position as Rector of Swanage he met Joseph Lancaster. Subsequently, Bell held various clerical positions and finally became Canon of Westminster. From an educational point of view, however, he lapsed into obscurity before dying in 1832. Lancaster, meanwhile, was succeeding in raising considerable sums of money from the aristocracy to help fund his expanding schools. Unfortunately, he spent as enthusiastically as he publicised, and was arrested for debt in 1807. In later years, his work became fragmented and his energies dissipated. Nevertheless, his ideas had been taken up in the New World, some Eastern European countries (including Russia), and in Western territorial possessions around the world.

Lancaster's influence had certainly been profound. However, the popularity of the system gradually waned over the years, not least because the state began to provide money for public education and teaching became increasingly professionalised. As with most innovations, it may well be that subsequent imitators lacked the attention to detail of its original proponents, and weaknesses were introduced into the system which made it less effective. It seems that the tutors themselves were given little specific training, acquiring their skills on an apprenticeship basis, and this may have proved inadequate in the long run.

SMALL SCHOOLS AND BIG CLASSES

We have already noted how large classes created the desirability, if not the necessity, of deploying at least some of the children as tutors or monitors. For many decades during the development of the state education system in Britain, classes of 50 and 60 pupils were very common, and it is very likely that some form of peer tutoring was deployed by some teachers, albeit on an informal and loosely structured basis, for at least some of the time. Equally, the one-teacher village school was once very common, although today it is usually only found in sparsely populated rural areas. In such schools, 'vertical grouping' is of necessity the favoured form of organisation; children from a wide range of age groups receiving instruction within a single room.

In such situations, the younger pupils of greater ability automatically have access to more advanced instruction, while less able pupils

15

automatically have access to frequent review and preview of material. Furthermore, the mixed-age classroom presents an ideal opportunity for older and more able pupils to assist younger and less able pupils with learning. Children of all ages are bound to mix socially to a greater extent than in a larger school.

In 1974 Allen and Devin-Sheehan surveyed the use of children as tutors in 110 rural schools which still functioned with a single teacher. Some form of tutoring was reported to take place on a fairly regular basis in 30 per cent of the schools, and in another 25 per cent there were similar informal arrangements. Most of the formal tutoring was on a one-to-one basis, although tutors frequently worked with more than one tutee during the week. Same sex and opposite sex pairings were equally frequent, while age differential ranged from 0 to 5 years. It seems likely that such arrangements had been in existence in these situations for some time, and would continue for the forseeable future.

THE TWENTIETH CENTURY

Whilst never widespread after the late 1800s, peer tutoring projects could still be found through into the twentieth century. Reigert (1916) describes the implementation of the Lancasterian system in the schools of New York City.

During the 1960s, there was to be a resurgence of interest in peer tutoring as attention in the United States focused on problems of under-achievement in the public schools. The 'individualisation of instruction' became a key phrase; it had proved very difficult to achieve purely via direct instruction from the relatively scarce resource which comprised teachers. From the middle of the decade onwards, workers developed possible solutions to national preoccupations based on the old ideas of Bell and Lancaster. The 'Tutorial Community' of Melaragno and Newmark incorporated the systematic and universal use of peers as mediators of instruction, with specification of professional teachers as managers of instruction rather than direct instructors, a programmed curriculum based on task-analysed behavioural objectives, and a training facility for those proposing to implement similar programmes elsewhere. This Tutorial Community was targeted on ethnic minority low-income populations. Melaragno and Newmark also took care to include a systematic evaluation in their programme development, and their work still makes inspiring reading. The first report appeared in 1969, but the most easily available source of programme description is a piece by Melaragno in the 1976 compilation by Allen, *Children as Teachers: theory and research on tutoring*.

At about the same time, Gartner *et al.* (1971) were documenting the resurgence of interest in modern peer tutoring, setting this in the context of the anti-poverty and compensatory education politics of the era, with most interest in the affective and attitudinal outcomes which might accrue from peer tutoring. These authors reported on, or referred to, hundreds of locally-based programmes revolving around some form of peer tutoring. By 1970, more than 200 school districts had adopted some type of *after-school* tutoring programme. By 1974, Melaragno was claiming that over 10,000 elementary schools had attempted some form of peer tutoring programme.

The return to popularity of peer tutoring in the United States inevitably had a ripple effect throughout the world. In 1975 Charconnet produced a UNESCO report reviewing various systems of peer tutoring with reference to their application in developing countries. Interest was also aroused in the United Kingdom, and a series of articles on peer tutoring appeared during the latter half of the 1970s in the *Times Educational Supplement*, the largest-circulation educational newspaper in the British Isles (Briggs 1974, 1975; Roper 1975; Doe 1980).

A significant event was the publication in 1979 by Sinclair Goodlad of a slim volume, *Learning by Teaching: an introduction to tutoring*, reviewing the field of peer tutoring. Goodlad made particular reference to his own programme in London wherein science undergraduates acted as infrequent but regular tutors to high school science pupils.

Goodlad had recently returned from a visit to the United States during which he investigated many peer tutoring programmes, and the North American connection is also strong with another major protagonist in the field of peer tutoring in the United Kingdom, Carol Fitz-Gibbon. Having done a great deal of work on peer tutoring while based at the Centre for the Study of Evaluation at the Graduate School of Education at the University College of Los Angeles, Fitz-Gibbon has worked for much of the 1980s from the School of Education at the University of Newcastle-upon-Tyne, generating (with associates and students) a number of innovative projects in high schools and other educational settings.

In the United Kingdom, the 1980s have been characterised by a massive growth of interest in parental involvement in children's reading (Topping and Wolfendale 1985). Out of this movement came the development of various semi-structured techniques of para-professional tutoring in reading, which appeared simple yet effective, were easily trained and could be applied without any need for specialised structured material. It was not long before two of these in particular ('Paired Reading' and 'Pause, Prompt and Praise') were perceived to be ideal vehicles for peer tutoring also. 'Peer Tutored Paired Reading', in particular, spread rapidly throughout the United Kingdom.

Thus, at a time when interest in peer tutoring in the United States may actually be beginning to wane (again), a tide of enormous enthusiasm for the promotion of parents in the role of reading tutors in the United Kingdom has given added momentum to the parallel development of peer tutoring in reading. Such developments will undoubtedly generalise to other curriculum areas. Reports of, and practical guides to, peer tutoring are increasingly appearing in the popular United Kingdom educational press (e.g. Bayliss 1986; Lee 1986; Topping 1987). Research on communication factors in the peer tutoring process is being undertaken at the University of Wales Institute of Science and Technology, and other substantial research is in hand. The concept of peer tutoring is being extended via the Paired Reading method to enable adults to tutor other adults in their natural environment. Hopefully the publication of this book will further accelerate developments in the field.

3

Examples and First Considerations

There are some inspiring examples in the literature of projects which have deployed peer tutoring on a large scale to very good effect. One of the most striking early examples was the 'Youth Tutoring Youth' programme in the United States. It started in 1967 in Newark, New Jersey and Philadelphia, recruiting 14- and 15-year-old children who were under-achieving in school, particularly in reading, to act as cross-age tutors for elementary school children from disadvantaged areas. In one location, para-professionals supervised the programme, while in another it was more closely linked in with the school system. In all, 200 tutors were involved, occupied with six hours of training and 16 hours of tutoring each week, for which they were paid US$1.25 an hour.

Startling increases in reading skills in both the tutors and the tutees became evident. Those involved in the project were impressed with the quality of care and enthusiasm shown by the tutors, particularly as demonstrated by the tutors' sustained interest, for only seven out of the 200 tutors dropped out.

Subsequently, Youth Tutoring Youth enjoyed considerable popularity. In 1969 it was operating in more than 60 cities and by 1972 this had spread to 450 centres of population. The benefits of peer tutoring which we have come to regard as commonplace were found to apply, and the tutors improved their own skills, developed more confidence, and attended school when not tutoring more regularly. The tutees also improved in confidence and, furthermore, often showed better behaviour in their own classrooms. There was also evidence of generalisation of tutoring behaviour, with the tutees beginning to adopt a helping relationship towards others in their school.

'HOMEWORK HELPERS'

Even earlier, in New York City (which has shown sustained interest in peer tutoring over the decades), a 'Homework Helper' programme commenced operation in 1963. Both high school and college students were recruited and employed as tutors for adolescent children in disadvantaged areas. Eventually more than 100 homework helper 'centers' were established in primary and secondary schools throughout the city. By the mid-1970s the programme was employing 1,000 tutors who were helping 5,000 tutees.

The programme aimed to provide direct help in a number of curriculum areas, as well as improving the study skills and work habits of participating tutees. A homework helper centre was staffed by a teacher in charge, one adult para-professional and about 15 tutors. Tutoring was usually available four days of the week, and tutees generally attended two days a week for sessions of two hours each. Again, tutors were paid.

This was a very large scale programme indeed, which demonstrated that given adequate organisation and support, tutoring can be operated on a widespread basis. However, it seems a long way from the modest aspirations of the average class-teacher, and so our attention will now increasingly turn to smaller scale projects.

THE TUTORIAL COMMUNITY

As we have seen, the programme at the Pacoima School in California was associated with the names of Melaragno and Newmark. It was an attempt to organise an entire school along peer tutoring lines. The Youth Tutoring Youth and Homework Helper programmes usually established peer tutoring as an after-school activity, but the idea of Melaragno and Newmark was to incorporate peer tutoring within the organisational fabric of the life of an elementary school.

The project developed as a 7-year rolling programme, eventually involving virtually all the school: 5-year-olds were tutored by 7- and 8-year-olds; 6-year-olds by children aged between 8 and 11 years, and the older children in the primary school received cross-age tuition from children imported from a nearby junior high school. All classes were involved in tutoring, either providing or receiving tutors.

As more and more classes became involved in peer tutoring, the timetabling problems became increasingly complex. Owing to this and other organisational stresses and strains, the use of peer tutoring at the school eventually faded away to a much more restricted level. Although well ahead of its time, innovative and exciting, and generating many very important research findings, the Tutorial Community experiment also demonstrates the dangers of biting off more than you can chew.

DEVELOPMENTS IN THE UNITED KINGDOM

In the early 1970s, interest in the field of Adult Literacy mushroomed in the United Kingdom. It had suddenly been noticed that an estimated two million adults were below the level of functional literacy. Funds were made available, energy was poured into publicity, recruitment and the production of materials, and (most significantly) the recruitment of volunteer para-professional tutors began. Over the subsequent decade, thousands of volunteer tutors were recruited, some of them working in the tutee's home, some of them working in centres. (Very much the same thing had happened in the United States ten years earlier, with the founding in 1962 of 'Literacy Volunteers of America'. The difference was in the scale of the problem — 27 million adults in the United States were estimated to be functionally illiterate, with 3.6 million having a marked problem with spoken English.) Thus peer tutoring on an adult-adult basis became established and taken for granted.

The seminal work of Goodlad and Fitz-Gibbon has been referred to earlier, and readers interested in their work should follow up the references directly for more detail. Goodlad's work with the 'Pimlico Connection' is not immediately relevant to our terms of reference here, involving as it did the importing of university undergraduates into high schools. Other workers in the United Kingdom have used peer tutors on a 'summer school' basis, the concept again having been drawn from the United States. A particularly interesting project in London was established by Community Service Volunteers, who utilised immigrant teenagers to tutor recently arrived Asian children in spoken English.

A number of high schools have used sixth formers to help younger pupils, both within the high school and in feeder primary schools. The range of activities such 'tutors' have been involved in is very wide, but there is a clear danger of their role deteriorating into merely that of 'teacher's helper'. Many high schools arrange for fifth-year pupils to help in local primary schools as part of a 'community service' element in their curriculum, but this option is usually reserved for the less academic children, and is often rather lacking in training for the tutors, structure, careful monitoring and a clear sense of purpose.

TUTORING IN READING

The peer tutoring movement was given an apposite motto by Alex Dickson (1972): 'Each One, Teach One'. He also wrote:

> The statistics which define the problem [of literacy] also indicate a means for easing it. If 15 per cent of the children have difficulty in reading, it follows that 85 per cent have acquired the skill. Here then is a human resource ready to hand — and it should surely be the function of remedial teachers to train and deploy this potential force of helpers.

Reading is *the* crucial basic skill area — it is the key to many other curriculum areas. Many peer tutoring programmes have focused upon the development of reading skills. In the United States, some of the best known reading tutoring programmes have adopted a highly structured format. Notable in this respect is the work of Ellson *et al*. (1968) and Niedermeyer (in Allen 1976, for example). To some extent this preoccupation with structure may reflect the view which was to be confirmed by empirical research that structured tutoring programmes tend to produce the best results, but it may also have reflected the rather mechanistic flavour of reading instruction in North America at the time (which has since been softened by an increasing emphasis on comprehension skills).

A structured tutorial system for reading has also been developed by von Harrison and his associates, based at Brigham Young University in Utah (e.g. von Harrison and Reay 1983). Six types of instructional tasks were required of the tutors: teaching letter names, teaching letter sounds, teaching blending of sounds, teaching decoding of new words which were phonically regular, teaching sight words (phonically irregular) and oral reading. Typically, each tutoring session would focus on a particular activity. The original pilot study was conducted when the children were not attending school, controlling for the effect of additional formal instruction. Tutoring sessions lasted 15 to 20 minutes each day for five days a week, continuing for six weeks. The programme proved effective; subsequently the tutorial system was developed to include the following components: supervisor's guide, training procedure, diagnostic pre-tests, 60-item prescriptive instructional sequence, home study materials for the tutor, blending exercises, record keeping forms, 25 decoding exercises, flash cards for letter sounds/letter names/digraphs/sight words, tutee progress reports to be passed to adults, chart to summarise learning gains, evaluative post-tests, reading exercises for teaching digraphs, sound pronunciation guide, ten story books, tutor assignment sheets, and the tutor's log which was to be maintained daily.

In later work, this tutorial system was often much more co-ordinated with ordinary classroom teaching. It was claimed that one adult could supervise approximately 50 tutors per day. Unit costs of implementing the programme were very low indeed compared to most types of individualised instruction. Materials were subsequently developed which applied to children through all the elementary grades in school. Materials were also devised to enable the system to be delivered by para-professional adult tutors. The programme has been applied in the field of adult literacy and the teaching of reading in Spanish. A range of other manuals, for teaching English as a second language, mathematics, writing and other skill areas has subsequently been produced.

Structured tutoring was noted by von Harrison to be 'not without its problems and limitations'. His system had been largely used in cross-age tutoring programmes where older pupils tutored younger pupils within a school setting. Results were consistently good, but von Harrison betrayed signs of frustration when, after 15 years of extensive research in the field, he wrote:

> Even though the benefits of cross-age tutoring have been demonstrated empirically, very few schools make use of pupils as tutors. Cross-age tutoring is fraught with problems, including the difficulty of matching timetables, movement of pupils, and possible public resentment where older pupils are 'missing' their lessons to tutor younger children. These problems are compounded if more than one school is to be involved.

Subsequently the workers in Utah decided to investigate the possibility of reorganising their reading materials and procedures so that they could be used in a single classroom in a true age-peer tutoring format. They carried out an investigation in a class of children aged 6 to 7 years, where the tutor and tutee roles were rotated regardless of the children's level of achievement, and this approach became known as 'Companion Study'. After these arrangements had been in operation for eight months, the score of the experimental group on a standard-ised test was twice that of the control group. It remains to be seen whether Companion Study, delivered by true age-peer tutoring within one classroom, is adopted any more readily by ordinary teachers at the grass roots.

BACK TO REALITY

This is all very well, you are thinking, *but* . . . big programmes funded and supported by university departments or central government may indeed be able to demonstrate the value of peer tutoring, but where does that leave the ordinary class teacher, in charge of their classroom but little else, with little time, even less money, and virtually zero outside help?

Teachers are very busy people. Society expects more and more of the education system, and the expanding curriculum is taking on the propensities of an exploding galaxy. Teachers are expected to do more and more with the same amount of time, the same amount of financial resources and within the same physical space. As expecta-tions of teachers rise, salaries do not seem to rise at the same rate, although the stress level does, with increased emphasis on profes-sional 'accountability'. In these circumstances, who but a fool would want to stick their neck out by trying to organise a peer tutoring pro-ject? And yet there is no future for peer tutoring (or any other educa-tional innovation) so long as it remains purely the province of univer-sity departments, special agencies and monied federal programmes. Only by incorporation in the daily life of many ordinary schools can peer tutoring take hold, have an impact on the learning of a large number of children, and in the long run endure at all. Interest in peer tutoring has waxed and waned in turn over the years. Given its effectiveness, if the method quietly slips again into oblivion a lot of children will be the losers.

For any method to be incorporated into the routine practice of class teachers, it is not enough that it merely demonstrates effectiveness. The method also has to be *cost*-effective, in terms of producing improved outcomes from the same amount of teacher time and energy and financial cost of resource materials. Even then there is no guarantee that a method will be widely adopted, unless there is an additional personal pay-off for the teacher. So it helps if a method is also fun to do. Fortunately, forms of peer tutoring have developed in recent years which fulfil these requirements.

If it isn't quick and easy, it doesn't get done. We are now reaching the point where peer tutoring can be made quick and easy, while remaining highly effective.

PAIRED READING

Paired Reading is a technique devised in the mid-1970s in the United Kingdom. It was originally intended for use by non-professional adults to accelerate the reading development of children with a reading disability. Subsequently, it has been used with children aged 5 to 15 years, and with adults. It has been used with non-readers and severely retarded readers, through to children who are above average readers. It has been used with those of all levels of cognitive ability, from mentally handicapped through to 'dyslexic' children of very high IQ. It appears to be startlingly effective.

Many of the elements of the Paired Reading technique have been around the reading scene for many years. What is different about it is that these elements are arranged in a coherent package which is readily disseminated, reliable in use and highly self-reinforcing. Using this method, the tutees select books of interest to them *irrespective of level of readability*. Thus no special materials are required, and the only organisational constraint is ensuring that tutees do not select books which are beyond the tutor's reading competence. This is easily achieved by teaching the pair a very simple readability check such as the 'five finger test'.[1] Conversation about the text, physical closeness and much praise for correct reading are emphasised. Correction procedures are kept extremely simple to ensure continuity of reading and availability of contextual clues. On difficult texts, tutor and tutee read out loud together, the tutor adapting to the tutee's natural speed. On easier texts, the tutee can signal for the tutor to be temporarily silent. The tutee continues reading alone, and when an error is made the tutor corrects it and then joins in reading together again.

Naturally, the technique in action is considerably more subtle and sophisticated than the brief outline given here. (Those seeking further details should refer to Topping, 1986. This is also the source of an up-to-date bibliography, which includes details of a large number of studies on peer tutoring applications, as well as the more common parent-tutored usage.) Paired Reading does require training and monitoring, but the training is brief and the monitoring is well within the compass of a single class teacher, provided the bulk of the tutoring is scheduled within class time.

WHERE TO START

As we approach the end of the twentieth century, it seems likely that a number of techniques and strategies will be developed for para-professional and peer tutoring which are naturalistic and lightweight but highly effective. To some extent peer tutoring has gone through the life cycle typical of many innovations. Initially a simple solution to a practical problem, perhaps peer tutoring has gone through a phase of being made over-technical and heavily 'professionalised', which may have served to put ordinary teachers off rather than encourage them. Reams of special materials and a ponderous organisational superstructure are unattractive to the average consumer in the educational methods market place. It is just as well that peer tutoring has demonstrated a long shelf life.

So where do *you* begin? What is to be your first small step into the strange new landscape of peer tutoring? As Goodlad (1979) put it, all you have to do is decide 'who is to teach what to whom and for what purpose, how and where, when and how often'.

Although it is possible to summarise the organisation of a peer tutoring project in one sentence, in the next two chapters we shall look at it in more detail. It will be as well to be prepared for every eventuality — after all, we want to be sure that your project will be successful. However, two simple rules will apply throughout — keep it small, and keep it simple. This is a grass roots survival skill we are cultivating.

NOTES

1. The tutor picks any page of the book at random, spreads the five fingers of one hand and places the fingertips on the text. If the tutor can accurately and fluently read the five words touched, the book is probably appropriate, but if there is difficulty in reading more than one of the five words, the book is too hard. If there is a problem with only one of the five words, the test is re-applied on a different page.

4

Organising a Project

There is no doubt that peer tutoring *can* work. That is unequivocally demonstrated by the research evidence. However, the evidence also shows that peer tutoring can *fail* to work, and failure you cannot afford. Careful planning is necessary to ensure that you are successful. This is particularly important if the project is a first venture.

THE CONTEXT

All children are different, and schools are even more different from each other. All successful peer tutoring projects have certain common elements, but each must be designed to fit comfortably within the ecology of a particular school at a particular time in its development.

Problems

Careful consideration should be given to potential problems which are specific to your individual establishment. There may be difficulties with a large proportion of ethnic minority pupils struggling to learn the majority language, or with massive reading problems in a particular age group, or a problem of pupils being so alienated from the aims of institutional education that they feel unable to play the part of a tutor comfortably. If you feel that standards in the school are, in general, lower than they should be, take especial care. The facilities, resources and curriculum in the school may be outdated or culturally inappropriate. The peer group may be divided into sub-groups, with poor relationships between them, and there may be a high incidence of behaviour problems coupled with generally low motivation in the students.

It is very important that peer tutor projects are not used to compensate for, and thereby perhaps disguise, fundamental weaknesses in the professional teaching or organisational infrastructure within a school.

Schools that have failed to organise many things are unlikely to have any greater success in successfully organising peer tutoring. It is also important that teachers do not see in peer tutoring a means of giving children extra practice while they remain under the direct supervision and control of the professional, as an *alternative* to the possibly more challenging development of involving the natural parents of the children in this exercise at home. Natural parents acting as helpers at home have great strengths in this role, as well as weaknesses, which are different from those of either peer tutors or professional teachers.

Support

Although it is possible to operate a peer tutor project in isolation within the confines of your own classroom, using peer tutors and tutees drawn from your own class group, some support from colleagues inside or outside the school is nevertheless highly desirable to maximise the chances of a successful first project. At the very least, the agreement of the head teacher to the project will be essential. If this is a new venture for the school, advice and support from colleagues in other, more experienced, local schools or specialist advisory agencies should be sought.

You may encounter four kinds of response from your professional colleagues towards your proposal. Some may feel that what you are intending is fundamentally wrong, and will go out of their way to express disapproval or be more tangibly obstructive. Others will be largely indifferent, but you may be grateful for the fact that they do not actually get in your way. The third kind of response is from those colleagues who express very positive attitudes towards your proposal, thinking it is 'a wonderful idea', and giving you much encouragement. This is all very well, and may make you feel good briefly, but you may find that these positive attitudes are not translated into practical help subsequently. The fourth and most valuable type of response comes from the colleague who is very interested and is prepared to offer you practical help, time and resources, perhaps as part of a learning exercise for themselves.

Throughout your planning, it will be most important that you are very clear about the delegation of any tasks relevant to your project. Where colleagues have agreed to undertake responsibility for specific aspects of organisation, this should constitute a cast-iron agreement. You are likely to find it useful to complete the Structured Planning Guide (Chapter 5) and circulate copies of it to colleagues who are supporting you so that they are fully aware of the organisational structure of the project — you may care to indicate *their* responsibilities with a big red pen!

Objectives

It is as well to be clear from the outset as to the objectives of the enterprise. Try to specify exactly what you hope to achieve, and try to write this down in observable, operational terms. Think of what you wish the children to be *doing* differently by the end of the project.

Different teachers will run peer tutor projects for very different purposes, and a success for one teacher could be construed as a failure by another teacher with different objectives and expectations. Objectives do need to be realistic. It is reasonable to expect both tutors and tutees to show increased competence in the curriculum area of the tutoring, and perhaps increased confidence and interest in that area. However, it is not reasonable to expect a brief project to make a major impact on a longstanding and widespread problem in the school. A degree of reasonable caution when setting objectives creates the possibility of being pleasantly surprised subsequently.

SELECTION AND MATCHING OF PARTICIPANTS

Background factors

All teachers have experienced the great variations in general maturity levels shown by classes in succeeding years. It would be particularly unwise to mount a project involving many children where the maturity of the majority to cope with the procedure is in grave doubt. In cases of uncertainty it is usually wisest to start with a small pilot project with a few of the most mature children in the class acting as tutors, to enable further tutors to be added to the project subsequently as a 'privilege'. Where the children have already been used to taking a degree of responsibility for independently guiding their own learning and/or working on co-operative projects in small groups, they may be expected to take to peer tutoring more readily.

Having said that, peer tutoring can in some circumstances improve peer group relationships and serve to develop social cohesiveness. Thus some teachers deliberately use it in situations where there *is* a lack of sharing, co-operation and mutual understanding in a group of children. However, the operation of projects of this sort is really the preserve of the more experienced project organiser, who has already run successful projects with more amenable groups of children.

Recruiting

In a project involving true age-peer tutoring within a single class, recruitment will be no problem. At least half of the class will readily volunteer when the nature of the exercise is briefly described. The project organiser must decide whether all the class are to be involved, or whether to start with a small group of volunteers and use them as a model of enjoyment which will persuade the rest of the class of the desirability of joining in a little later. There is some advantage in leaving the more diffident children to consider their decision at leisure, since a definite positive commitment will definitely get the project off to a better start. Public demonstration is certainly the most potent form of advertising.

In cross-age and cross-institution projects, recruitment is always more complex, and publicity inevitably more difficult to arrange. Again, it is as well to work in the first instance with well-motivated participants. Start small, and if the project works at all some momentum should be developed which inevitably draws in other children. Where tutees or tutors do not already exist as a naturalistic group, they may need to be approached individually. In this circumstance, a clear form of words should be prepared which is used consistently in all invitations, to dispel any anxieties which may be aroused by the initial approach. Contact should preferably be made personally, but some project co-ordinators have utilised written invitations, and publicity by advertisements on posters and handbills, and in newspapers and magazines. The impact of transmission of good news by word of mouth through the 'grapevine' should not be underestimated.

Age

If you intend to use tutors who are considerably older than the tutees, unless you are fortunate enough to teach a vertically grouped or mixed-age class, you are likely to find the organisation of the project considerably more complicated, particularly if the tutors are to be 'imported' from another school. Remember that an age differential between tutors and tutees is probably of less significance than an ability differential. Any cross-age tutoring arrangement will almost inevitably create difficulties of matching timetables and movement of pupils. Although you may find strong views among your colleagues and indeed the children themselves as to the acceptability of either arrangement, perhaps with strong preference being expressed for one, remember that both true age-peer and cross-age tutoring tend to be equally effective, although there is some evidence that where the ability (and therefore often the age) of the tutor is substantially greater than that of the tutee, the *tutee* may be expected to benefit more, although this may be at the cost of the *tutor* benefiting somewhat less.

Numbers

Most peer tutoring is done in a one-to-one situation, but it can occur in small groups of three, four or five children. If this latter arrangement is to be established, it is important to make the rules for the group and the role of tutor or 'leader' very clear, or the children may spend more time bickering about organisation than actually getting on with the task in hand.

It is always as well to start with a small number of children in the first instance. Resist any temptation to include 'just one more', or before you know where you are the whole thing will become unmanageable. Particularly for a first venture, it is important to be able to monitor closely a small number of children. Do not worry about those who have to be 'excluded'. They can have a turn later, or be incorporated into the project as your organisation of it becomes more fluent and automatic. Besides, if any evaluation is to be carried out, it will be useful also to check the progress of a comparison group of children who have *not* been involved in the peer tutoring. Most of the research work on peer tutoring has been done with pairs rather than small tutor groups, and the former arrangement may prove organisationally more simple, the more satisfying for the 'pairs', and promote a maximum of time on task.

Ability

The range of ability in the children is a critical factor in selection and matching of tutors and tutees. A widely used rule of thumb is to keep a differential of about two years in attainment between tutors and tutees (unless operating some form of 'reciprocal' tutoring). When drafting an initial matching on the basis of ability, it is possible to rank the available children in terms of their attainment in the curriculum area of tutoring, draw a line through the middle of the list separating tutors at the top and tutees at the bottom, and then pair the most able tutor with the most able tutee, and so on. In some projects, the alternative approach has been taken of pairing the most able tutor with the least able tutee, but this sometimes creates the situation where the gap in ability is so wide that little stimulation is available from the tutoring materials for the tutor. On the other hand, if a minimal differential in ability is not maintained, and the tutor's abilities approximate to those of the tutee, then very little gain in attainment can be expected from the tutees, except those resulting from increased time on task.

Relationships

The children's ability is by no means the only factor which must be taken into account. Pre-existing social relationships in the peer group must also be considered. To pair children with their 'best friends' of the moment may not be a good idea in all cases, particularly as the friendship may be of short duration, but obviously it would be undesirable to pair a child up with another child with whom there is a pre-existing poor relationship. Especial care is necessary with the pairings in cases where tutees are known to be of particularly timorous or over-dependent personality, or tutors are known to be rather dominant or authoritarian by nature.

Participant preference

It is usually desirable to take the individual preferences of the participants themselves into account in some way, and some children may surprise you with the maturity they show in selecting a tutor they think would be effective in this role. However, to allow completely free child selection of tutor is likely to generate a degree of chaos, not least because some tutors will be over-chosen, while others may not be chosen at all, quite apart from the question of maintaining the requisite differential in reading ability. One possible compromise is to have the tutees express their preferences in writing in a 'secret ballot', with each tutee allowed to express up to three choices. In cross-age projects where the potential tutors may be unfamiliar to the tutees, some project organisers have had the tutees express three preferences based on photographs of the potential tutors. Tutees may be encouraged to express negative as well as positive preferences.

The sex balance in the class can present a problem, particularly if there are more girls than boys, since initially many boys express reluctance at the prospect of being tutored by a girl. Needless to say, this reluctance often disappears fairly quickly where the teacher allocates a female tutor to a male tutee and instructs them to get on with it, but the unfortunate tutee may still have great difficulty justifying what is going on to his friends in the playground. However, one effect of this kind of cross-sex tutoring may well be to improve relationships and dispel stereotypes. There is some evidence that organising a project with girls as tutors and boys as tutees is a particularly effective combination in terms of attainment gains for all concerned.

Many of these social considerations apply equally to the establishment of pairings of mixed race. Peer tutoring can offer a focus for social contact between children who might otherwise be inclined to avoid each other owing to completely unfounded assumptions or anxieties.

Standby tutors

It is always worthwhile to nominate a 'supply tutor' or two, to ensure that absence from school of the usual tutor can be covered. Children acting as spare tutors need to be particularly stable, sociable and competent in the curriculum area of the project, since they will have to work with a wide range of tutees. However, do not worry about imposing a burden on the spare tutors, as they may be expected to benefit the most in terms of increased ability. In cross-age or cross-institution projects, in which it may be more difficult to ascertain regular and frequent tutoring contact, more standby tutors may need to be appointed. If there is a danger of any volunteer tutors dropping out before the end of the project, there are again implications for nominating standbys to fill this sort of gap.

Parental agreement

The question of parental agreement often arises in connection with peer tutor projects. Experience shows that involvement in such a project is usually sufficiently interesting for the children as to result in many of them mentioning it at home. This can result in some parents getting very strange ideas about how teachers are using their time and how taxes are being spent. It is thus usually desirable for a brief note from school to be taken home by both tutors and tutees, explaining the project very simply, underlining that participation is purely voluntary, and reassuring parents that the project will have both academic and social benefits for tutors as well as tutees. The necessary minimum of information should be given, couched in a simple and straightforward but reassuring format. (See 'Handout for Parents', in Chapter 8, which is intended to serve this purpose. It may be photocopied for immediate use.)

Incentives

Some peer tutoring projects, particularly in North America, have incorporated some form of payment or tangible reward for tutors. Quite apart from the question of availability of finance to support this, such an approach is unlikely to find widespread favour. The majority of organisers of peer tutor projects prefer to rely on the intrinsic motivation of tutors and tutees alike. There is strong evidence that both tutors and tutees in a well-organised project not only benefit academically but also develop rewarding social relationships and actually enjoy themselves. There is good evidence that the addition of extrinsic or artificial reinforcers in a situation where adequate intrinsic motivation already exists can have damaging effects on the latter, and is at best cost-ineffective. Some project organisers do utilise badges of identification, certificates of merit and effort, and very small 'prizes' such as pens, but these have much more import at the social psychological level as a token of esteem and an indicator of belonging than as any form of tangible reward.

CURRICULUM AREA

Reading is the most popular curriculum area for the establishment of peer tutor projects, and within this there is little doubt that oral reading is the most emphasised aspect. Some projects have focused on word recognition skills and others on decoding strategies. A small number have concerned themselves with more complex and abstract issues, such as comprehension of written material, while a few have gone beyond this into the area of literary criticism.

The mathematics area has also been a popular target. Many projects have concerned themselves with fairly routine drill in mathematical facts, but this runs the risk of becoming boring for both tutor and tutee. Other projects have sought to apply peer tutoring principles to much more abstract concept development in the mathematical area, dealing with tasks such as sorting and conservation.

The language area also lends itself to this kind of approach, and various aspects have been peer tutored. Some projects have concentrated on expansion of vocabulary and understanding of complex concepts. Others have been designed to increase the volume and quality of expressive language in the tutee, often utilising some form of game format. More didactic projects have incorporated the target areas of punctuation, grammar, and capitalisation.

A closely associated curriculum area is that of spelling. Here again some projects have emphasised drill, with much rote learnng and re-checking of wordlists. Other projects have concerned themselves more with generalised spelling skills, dealing with phonically regular spelling by the standard strategies and irregular 'sight' words via some sort of mnemonic or rule-oriented approach.

Writing skills have likewise been approached in a variety of ways. There is relatively little reference in the literature to peer tuition of the early stages of handwriting skill, including such aspects as letter formation, but simple structured programmes are available in this area and it may be that this kind of work will be developed. With more creative writing, projects have certainly developed forms of peer 'editing' and 'critical review', and this could clearly also include oversight of spelling accuracy in the context of continuous writing rather than an artificial test situation. Equally, peer tuition of aspects of punctuation, capitalisation and grammar could be included if desired. However, it would probably be unwise to ask peer tutors to address themselves to issues of literary merit, formal structure *and* spelling in the course of reviewing a single piece of writing, unless they had a very clear structure for so doing.

An area of curriculum which merits further attention and expansion generally is that of the teaching of thinking skills and problem solving strategies. Peer tutoring may present an ideal vehicle for such an expansion. Materials are easily produced in simple written or

35

diagrammatic form, and kits of games are equally available. This is an area in which you can be assured that both tutor and tutee will be unable to tick along on half throttle, since every task will by definition be novel.

Peer tutoring has also been applied to sophisticated areas of the high school curriculum, such as physical science, social science and foreign languages (including French, German and Spanish). In the latter case, the project organiser can again be assured that both tutor and tutee will be engaged in a highly useful activity, and indeed peer tutoring may be the only way in which students of foreign languages can have sufficient oral practice in the context of the ordinary classroom. This presents an interesting parallel to the situation with the development of reading skills.

A major issue that presents itself here is the question of the relationship of the 'peer tutoring curriculum' to the mainstream or core curriculum in the school as a whole. For ease of organisation, project organisers may wish to use packaged kits of materials for the peer tutor project, but care must be taken that these materials not only do not conflict with the rest of the school curriculum, but also (preferably) that the peer tutor materials support and integrate with the main strands of curricular experience for all children.

MATERIALS

Structure

There is some evidence that peer tutoring is more effective in raising attainment when structured materials are used than in other circumstances. Certainly, the availability of carefully sequenced materials which take tutees step-by-step, ensuring success along the way, may be easier for tutors to follow reliably and may reduce the need for lengthy and complex training.

However, considerable costs may be involved in the preparation of such materials, or in the purchase of existing structured packages where these are relevant and available. Also, project organisers should beware of the introduction of so much structure that the responses of tutor and tutee alike become rigid and mechanical. Materials that are too highly structured may inhibit tutor initiative and reduce the opportunities for tutors to participate creatively. Complex structured materials also suffer from automatic inhibition of generalisation, in that their restricted availability may prevent additional spontaneous tutoring from occurring in the project participants' own free time.

Much of the early work in the area showed high effectiveness with structured materials delivered by tutors in a pre-specified and structured manner, but evidence on generalisation and maintenance of gains was not always presented. In more recent years, there has been more emphasis on the utilisation of structured *techniques* which are of broad-spectrum applicability to a wide range of materials which need not be structured and are readily available.

Difficulty

A related question concerns the control of the difficulty level of the materials. In a very highly structured sequence, some form of placement test may be necessary to determine at what point the tutee should commence. Subsequently, in this situation, mastery of each task determines progression to the next, so the sequence is predetermined, if not the speed of progress. Other projects have worked on the basis of drafting individual educational plans for each tutee, implying pre-specification of a learning sequence for each student.

Other approaches which are less dependent on highly structured materials have allowed some choice by the tutee and/or tutor from a variety of materials which are nevertheless compressed to be within a band of difficulty. More recently still, techniques have been developed which allow tutors and tutees free access to materials of uncontrolled difficulty. In these cases, tutors and tutees have often been taught skills to enable them to choose mutually interesting materials at an appropriate level of difficulty for both. Choice by negotiation between the tutorial pair is the general rule in these circumstances.

However good the training in choosing appropriate materials may be, some of the children in the project will be slow to acquire the requisite skills. This may largely be because they have lacked practice in this respect in the past, and have become over-dependent on teacher direction. Thus, those members of the project who have not developed the requisite choosing skills after the first two or three weeks of the project may need further gentle encouragement or guidance from the project co-ordinator.

Some projects have gone further down the road towards independent control of learning by vesting the responsibility for choice entirely with the tutee. (Of course, in all circumstances the difficulty of the material must be controlled to be within the level of the *tutor's* competence.) Unless the teaching of choosing skills is particularly effective, this can result in episodes of inefficient tutoring, and runs the risk of the tutor becoming bored, so some degree of negotiation and compromise is usually seen as desirable — and is of course entirely in the spirit of 'co-operative learning'.

Availability and sources

Materials are expensive, in cost to buy, in time to arrange and collect loans, in time to devise, in time to manufacture and in cost of raw materials. Peer tutoring works by promoting increased time spent on task, and the speed of progress through materials can often be much more rapid than is normal in ordinary classroom teaching. This can create an embarrassment for the project co-ordinator, who can find the stock of relevant and available materials rapidly exhausted.

In some circumstances it may be possible for the tutorial pairs to make some materials, if not for themselves than perhaps for other tutorial pairs, but if this is done the project organiser needs to be satisfied that such joint manufacturing is in itself serving an educational purpose. Carefully structured materials are already available in kit form, perhaps most notably from Science Research Associates (SRA), but these packages are extremely expensive, and are likely to be beyond the reach of many project organisers, unless they are already available in school and not being used for another purpose, or can be loaned on a short-term basis from a library or other establishment.

Many projects operate on the basis of a collection of paper durables, but if you wish to extend into peer tutoring in some mathematical areas (for instance), the availability of expensive hardware such as computers or other micro-electronic devices may be highly desirable. A further consideration is the cost of consumables, and some projects involve the using up of a substantial stock of paper, pencils, worksheets etc. Particularly in the area of peer tutored reading, the bringing in to the tutorial situation of materials gathered by the participants from outside of the school may be possible, and books or magazines may be obtained from participants' homes and local public libraries.

Access

A school may pride itself on the volume of relevant materials which it possesses, and forget to pay close attention to how easily the tutorial pairs can actually have access to the material. In reading projects, it is not enough for the school to contain a large number of books, it is also necessary for the children to have very regular and frequent access to them. This is particularly so when the speed of progression through materials is typically more rapid in the peer tutoring situation than is expected by teaching staff. It may be logistically easier to mount a special additional collection in some convenient area for access by the tutorial pairs.

Project co-ordinators should also consider the relationship of the project to other school facilities (such as a book shop), the desirability of arranging visits to the local public library, and any other events relevant to the curriculum area of the tutoring project which are arrangeable or spontaneously occurring. It is necessary to be clear about which member of the tutorial pair takes the initiative on access to materials — is this the job of the tutor or tutee or both? Do members of tutorial pairs need some form of special pass to give them access to otherwise forbidden areas of the school to facilitate easy access to materials? If high status is enjoyed by the tutoring project (as is usually the case), this kind of free access is seen by the children as a privilege and is very rarely abused.

Progression criterion

Highly structured materials may have the advantage of inbuilt mastery criteria which make it very clear when the tutorial pair are to move on to the next section of the prescribed materials. At the other end of the spectrum, where tutorial pairs are allowed a free choice of materials irrespective of difficulty level, as in Paired Reading projects, the issue of progression criterion does not arise, since a variability in difficulty level from week to week or day to day is usual, and accommodated by the tutorial technique.

In the grey area between these two extremes, issues may arise of who determines on the basis of what criteria when the tutee is (a) ready and (b) willing to move on to a fresh set of material, either covering different conceptual content or of more advanced difficulty. The specification of progression criteria will usually be seen by teachers as requiring their professional expertise, but this can be significantly time consuming. Those techniques and materials which have inbuilt progression criteria or have dispensed with the need for progression criteria altogether save the teacher valuable time in this respect.

Records

It is almost certain that some form of records will be kept of the tutoring process, whether by the project organiser, the tutors, the tutees or some combination of these. Again, some cost is involved in terms of time for preparation, materials used, and time and space for storage and dispensation. There may be official forms constituting record sheets or cards, progress reports to complete, or probes and tests to be accessed at the appropriate moment. Clear specification is necessary of what recording materials are necessary, who is responsible for keeping the records safe and available, who completes them, who obtains them from stock when required, and who replenishes the stock as it is depleted.

CONTACT

Time

A basic decision is whether the tutoring is to occur wholly in class time, wholly in the children's break time, or in a combination of both. If the tutoring is to occur entirely in class time, it can be kept under teacher supervision, but will usually require timetabling, which may rob the exercise of a degree of desirable spontaneity. If the tutoring is to occur in the children's break time, some very mature pairs can be left to make their own arrangements, but this is a much greater imposition on tutors and tutees alike, and the momentum of the project may begin to peter out as the novelty begins to wear off. Some timetabling may thus be necessary even during the children's break time, so that the size and nature of the commitment involved is visible to all from the outset.

The best arrangement may well be to schedule a basic minimum of contact during class time, but make available the possibility for tutoring pairs to negotiate further sessions in their own break time according to their own levels of enthusiasm. Some projects have arranged for contact after school, or indeed before school starts in the morning. Such arrangements are of course highly constrained by the transport arrangements for homeward-bound children and should only be attempted if the enthusiasm of the participants is high. Some American projects have worked a system of after-school tutoring supported by financial incentives for the tutors, but this is expensive and certainly more complex to organise.

Place

Finding the physical space to accommodate the pairs can be a problem. In a cross-age tutor project within one school, particularly where two full classes are involved, it is possible for half of the pairs to work in the tutees' classroom and the other half in the tutors' classroom. Finding physical space for the tutoring to occur during break times may be considerably more difficult if there are problems of break time supervision and/or children are not allowed access to classrooms. Clearly, a positive social atmosphere is more likely to be fostered if the children have adequate personal space and are comfortable during their tutoring. An ambience with a degree of informality is therefore preferable, but the situation should not be so informal as to incorporate many distractions from the tutoring process. A much used leisure area is therefore unlikely to be satisfactory.

Noise too may well be a problem. In true age-peer tutoring within one classroom, the noise generated by 15 or more pairs of enthusiastic children reading together is quite considerable. This is exacerbated in an open-plan school, and may generate complaints from other classes who are pursuing a more formal curriculum. It is worth checking the degree of noise transmission in advance, in order to be prepared for this type of complaint. The availability of an adequate quantity of comfortable seating can also be problematic. Even in a simple reading project, to find enough chairs which may be situated side by side and are reasonably comfortable for both participants might not be easy. Where the peer tutoring curriculum is more formal and incorporates some paper and pencil work, the availability of tables also has to be considered.

In cross-age tutor projects, the noise and inconvenience generated by the movement of pupils from one location to another is also relevant. This is in addition to the other complications of cross-age tutor projects in terms of matching timetables, etc. Seating arrangements need to be such that the mobility of professional supervisors will not be impaired. In cross-institution peer tutoring, the 'imported' students will need to be briefed about the layout of the building, and shown round — this is, of course, ideally done by the host students.

Duration

Each individual tutoring period should last for a minimum of 15 minutes. Little worthwhile can occur in less time than this, after you have allowed for lack of punctuality and general settling down. If it is possible for those who so desire to continue for 20 or 30 minutes, this is advantageous. Tutoring sessions of 30 minutes certainly seem to be the most common period found in the literature. It might be possible for the minimum of 15 minutes to occur just before a natural break time, and there could be provision for the tutoring pairs continuing into their own break time if they so desire. Tutoring periods as long as 60 minutes are very unusual, and it would be rare for tutoring to be scheduled as long as this. It is always better to leave the tutoring pair less than exhausted at the end of their joint experience, in order that they will come to their next session with positive attitudes and high energy levels.

Frequency

To ensure that a project has a significant impact, the frequency of tutorial contact needs to be at least three times per week. Contact frequency of this order is very commonly found in the literature. However, if four or five weekly contacts can be arranged, so much the better. Children involved in peer tutor projects rarely object to daily tutoring, as most of them find it interesting and rewarding. Some pairs may organise their own impromptu sessions in their own break time whether the teacher likes it or not! Some projects have incorporated twice daily contacts, but this is rare. Although the literature suggests that the greater the frequency of tutoring sessions, the more impact a project is likely to have, nevertheless a point of diminishing marginal returns may be found. It has also been suggested that four hours spent tutoring per week will guarantee evidence of effectiveness, irrespective of technique and materials used, but most teachers will be balancing the various contributory factors to success in a more subtle way than this.

42

Project period

The project should be launched with reference to an initial fixed period of commitment. It is useful for both tutors and tutees to be clear about what they are letting themselves in for, and how long a course they need to be able to sustain. Additionally, the literature suggests that short-term projects tend to generate bigger effect sizes. Although this may be merely due to capitalisation on sheer novelty, teachers are much less inclined than academics to be dismissive about the value of the Hawthorne Effect (the tendency for the introduction of any new form of organisation to produce short-term increments in performance). Apart from the desirability of keeping children hungry for 'a little more', constraints on resources may dictate a short initial experimental period. Particularly in a situation where not all members of a class are involved, there may be a strain on professional staffing in terms of the need to supervise two separate groups of children who in the normal course of events would all be in one classroom under the supervision of one teacher.

So a minimum project period of six weeks is suggested, since it would barely be possible to discern significant impact in less time than this. Popular project periods are eight weeks and ten weeks, which fit comfortably within an average term or semester, and it is not usually desirable to fix a period of longer than twelve weeks for an *initial* commitment. It will be much better to review the project at the end of a short initial period, and to obtain feedback from the participants and evaluate the outcomes, and at that stage make conscious joint decisions about improvements or future directions. One thing to definitely avoid is letting the whole thing dribble on interminably until it runs out of steam.

TECHNIQUE

Packaged techniques

There are a number of techniques for peer tutoring which have been carefully and coherently organised into easily deliverable packages. Examples of these in the reading area include 'Reading Together', 'Paired Reading', and 'Pause Prompt Praise'. All of these are designed to be relatively simple albeit structured techniques which are applicable to a wide range of materials.

In the United States, packaged techniques have sometimes tended to be even more highly structured, incorporating not only structured tutoring techniques but also highly structured teaching materials. Such programmes would include the various forms of 'Programmed Tutoring', 'Companion Study', and the 'SWRL Programme', etc. (See 'Practical Manuals and Kits' in Chapter 8.)

With reference to reading comprehension, teachers may wish to experiment with the 'Predict, Question, Summarise and Clarify' technique (Palincsar and Brown 1986) or 'SQ3R' methods. In the mathematics area, the structured nature of the curriculum particularly lends itself to highly sequenced materials. To some extent this is also true of the spelling area, but both can easily lapse into mindless drill. An interesting variant in the spelling area is the para-professional technique known as 'Cued Spelling'. (See under 'Paired Reading' in Chapter 8.)

There are obviously considerable attractions in using a pre-defined and packaged tutoring technique, since one may build on the experience of previous workers and avoid unnecessary anxiety about the appropriateness of what one is attempting. Additionally, there will usually be a background of research evidence from other workers with which one may compare one's own results. The use of a pre-existing package is thus strongly recommended for those embarking on their first peer tutoring project. Once experience in the field has been gained, exotic and esoteric new techniques can be the subject of individual experimentation. Consult Chapter 8 (Resource Materials) for sources of full details of these techniques.

Precision teaching and behavioural methods

In the United States much of the early work on peer tutoring in reading required the tutors to present words, phrases or sentences on flash cards to the tutees, apply some simple correction procedure in the event of tutee error, and reward tutee success with praise, points or other tokens. From a current European perspective, this kind of procedure is likely to be seen as mechanistic and unappealing. Certainly such techniques would appear to place a greater imposition on the altruism of the tutors than do more naturalistic techniques, and seem intuitively less likely to generate academic gains in the tutors. Given a clear enough structure, there is not necessarily any need for tutors to be particularly able or mature to use these techniques, but these latter requirements may be highly desirable if tutors are to use the techniques with great subtlety and sensitivity. From the European point of view, it is more likely that such methods will be favoured for use with those with severe difficulties or who are mentally handicapped.

Nevertheless, the framework of Precision Teaching, barely discernible in the early methods used in the United States, has the virtue of being applicable to virtually any area of the curriculum, given a little imagination on the part of the programme originator. (For information on Precision Teaching, see Topping and Wolfendale 1985, Branwhite 1986, and Formentin and Csapo 1980 — in order of complexity.) However, Precision Teaching is basically a framework wherein which teaching objectives can be delivered and their achievement systematically evaluated. Within this framework, particular techniques for actually improving the tutee's mastery of specific objectives are not prescribed — this is left to the capabilities of the tutor.

Where a more overtly behavioural method is in use, implying not only detailed checking of achievement of objectives but also the dispensation of tangible or token reinforcement for achievement of those objectives, it will be extremely important that the criteria for correct performance are carefully specified. There is nothing worse than a tutee who feels that the tutor is being unduly 'harsh' in their interpretation of what constitutes a correct response. (Where only social reinforcements are on offer, this has less importance than where countable indices of success such as tokens are in use.) Quite apart from the question of the impact on the *intrinsic* motivation of the tutee, such programmes raise questions about the effectiveness of tangible reinforcement in the long term. The same tangible reinforcer dispensed routinely and massively can produce a saturation effect, and the organisational problems of introducing constant variety may be considerable. The token system is of course intended to get round this problem, but this equally brings its own administrative complexities in relation to the system for exchanging tokens for subsequent tangibles, activities or other treats.

General teaching skills

Some workers have tried to avoid the rigidity sometimes inherent in very highly structured materials and techniques by attempting to train tutors in much more general teaching skills. These could include how to present a task, how to give clear explanations, how to demonstrate certain tasks and skills, how to prompt or lead pupils into imitating those skills, how to check on tutee performance, how to give feedback on performance, how to identify consistent patterns of error or problem in tutee responses, and how to develop more intensive remedial procedures for those patterns of error.

It is fairly immediately obvious that this range of skills is considerably sophisticated, and would usually only be associated with professional work. Nevertheless, particularly where relatively able and mature tutors are being used, ambitious programmes have taken such wide ranging training on board. Various workers have attempted to categorise the requisite skills involved in a number of ways. An obvious separation is between the tutoring skills needed to establish good interpersonal relationships, tutoring skills which are specific to the teaching materials in hand, and skills requisite to systematic checking and record keeping.

The attitudes the tutor brings to the task are obviously very important, and some workers have dwelt on creating a positive orientation or 'set' to tutoring in the tutors from the outset. In some programmes, tutors have been carefully given a complete overview of the structure of the various components and the aims of the project. The importance of positive attitudes in encouraging regular attendance has been emphasised, and considerable attention given to means of establishing good rapport with tutees and stimulating positive tutee motivation. Sometimes information about the problems of tutees has been given to the tutors in order to develop empathy. Equally, tutors have sometimes been advised about the dangers of feeling too 'sympathetic' towards the tutees, and falling too readily into the trap of providing unconscious prompts and excessive help which might foster over-dependence.

Ways of giving clear instructions without unnecessary elaboration or the use of difficult vocabulary have been included in some projects. The appropriate point at which to resort to demonstration of the requisite skill may be covered, as may precise details of how and when prompts or guides in practice should be used. Tutors have been trained in how to give systematic instruction, how to observe closely the tutee response, how to give encouraging but accurate feedback regarding the tutee response, and how to respond differentially to different kinds of tutee response. Other relevant tutor skills have included the identification of areas where the tutee needs extra help, systematic mastery checking, record keeping, the issue of token reinforcement, the ability to deal with 'take-homes' and home back-up reinforcers, the ability to manage and refer to any contracts which have been made in respect of the project, and the ability to discuss the progress of the tutee with the project organiser or other supervisor, and the tutee themselves.

All of this sounds extremely complicated and ambitious, as indeed it is, but care must be taken not to underestimate the abilities of the tutors, potential or actual. Many tutors may be well versed in a variety of helping behaviours in other environments, and for many of them training and tutoring behaviours will merely require the shaping of more precise skills from existing repertoires of behaviour, rather than instruction from a baseline of no skill at all. Clearly, however, the demands of this kind of generalist approach are not inconsiderable, both cognitively and socially, and the introduction of such an approach with young or relatively less able children should be left very much to the experienced peer tutoring project organiser.

With younger or less able children, something more like routine drill may not be a bad place to start, by virtue of its simplicity, although it can rapidly become fairly boring and does not have the social psychological impact of more complex forms of tutoring technique. However, when (for instance) deploying mentally handicapped students as tutors for each other, some form of drill would have its attractions. Needless to say, the categories referred to above are in no way mutually exclusive, and combinations of aspects of these methods may well be desirable and necessary for a successful project.

Correction procedure

Errors imply failure, and failure creates stress, and stress can produce a negative reaction in the tutee, and possibly also in a tutor who feels that errors are an indication of incompetence on their part. To avoid irritation, frustration and disharmony in the tutoring relationship, all techniques must include some form of pre-specified error correction procedure. Whatever this is, it needs to be quick, simple and consistently applicable, easy and non-stressful for both children. If in doubt, the standard simple Direct Instruction model (Topping and Wolfendale 1985) is a good one to fall back on. This stipulates that whenever the tutee makes an error, the tutor signals (usually non-verbally) the error, demonstrates or models the correct response, leads or prompts the tutee to imitate the correct response, checks that the tutee can produce the correct response unaided, and at some later point re-checks that the tutee can still emit the correct response on request. This kind of framework can be applied to almost any curriculum area and any kind of mistake, and has the advantage of not leaving the tutee to struggle for any significant length of time before help and support is forthcoming.

Praise

If well-considered error correction procedures are carefully and consistently deployed by the tutors, much of the aggravation which can arise when non-professionals try to teach children will be avoided. However, merely taking the latent heat out of a relationship is not enough if the result is bland neutrality. We would wish the tutors to go further than this, and specification is needed of the nature, frequency and circumstances for usage of praise in the tutoring relationship. It is useful to specify some sort of minimum frequency with which praise should be deployed, but even more important to give a clear indication of those circumstances where it should always be used. In Paired Reading, for instance, praise is specified as requisite whenever the child correctly reads a long word where the tutor expected an error, and whenever the tutee self-corrects before tutor intervention.

Many tutors find that the giving of verbal praise does not come naturally to them, and they may need considerable practice and feedback in this specific aspect before an adequate level of performance is achieved. In training, the verbal and non-verbal aspects of praise should be emphasised, since the use of routine praise words in a boring monotone will not have the desired effect. In addition, in some tutoring relationships the use of a pat on the back, a pat on the head or some other gesture may serve to add variety to the social reinforcement. Some tutors have a very restricted vocabulary of praise words, and part of tutor training could include a listing of appropriate vocabulary. In cases of doubt, tutors can be encouraged to discuss this with their tutees, since the latter may be able to generate more culturally appropriate praise vocabulary. In addition to verbal and non-verbal praise, the record keeping inherent in the project organisation may include an element of written praise from both tutors and supervising professionals.

Tutoring involves a very subtle social process. Some programmes take pains to instruct tutors in the establishing of an initial rapport, giving hints on the initiation of conversation, discovering something about the tutee and their interests, the importance of revealing things about oneself in order that the tutee may do likewise, and so on. It is obviously important for the tutor to learn about the interests of the tutee in a variety of areas, especially since discovery of a shared interest will do much to cement the bond between the two. In addition to the verbal and non-verbal social skills involved in praising, the importance of aspects of behaviour such as physical proximity, eye contact and posture may be incorporated in initial training for tutors.

Trouble shooting

In a first project, particularly when using a non-standard technique, the project organiser may not be well prepared for the sorts of difficulties which do arise in tutoring relationships and the tutoring process. Once some experience has been gained, it is worthwhile producing some sort of simple directory of common problems with some indication of how these may be solved. Even if this is not made available in written form to the tutors as a training resource, it will serve as a very handy reference for the project organiser.

You may rest assured that there will be constant additions to the collection with every subsequent project, for no projects are quite the same and certainly no children are quite the same. One advantage of using a standard packaged technique for a first project is that clues about likely problems will be found in the literature, together hopefully with some indications of solutions which other people have found effective. Either way, it will be worthwhile making clear at the outset that problems may arise which are *not* the fault of either tutor or tutee. If this is not done, the tutor or tutee may be inclined when difficulties are first encountered to either blame themselves for the problem or to blame their tutorial partner — both of these circumstances are highly undesirable.

It is as well for the tutorial pair to work on the assumption that if the relationship or process is not working satisfactorily, there is something wrong with the design of the materials or the design of the technique, and they should seek professional advice immediately in order that appropriate adjustments can be made. As well as communicating this assumption to the tutors and tutees, it will be as well for the project co-ordinator also to make it an essential foundation of *their* conceptual framework. If the tutoring is not working, it is not the fault of the children, it is because you haven't organised it correctly!

TRAINING

Staff training

Before teachers set out to train children in particular procedures, it is clearly important that teachers *themselves* are well versed in the methods to be used. All the relevant professionals need to be fully conversant not only with the technique in use but also the materials, especially where special or structured materials are to be an essential feature of the project. Even for professional teachers (or perhaps especially for professional teachers), there is great danger in assuming that you can learn enough about a technique from written or audio-visual information to be able to train tutors and tutees well. There is no substitute for being taught how to do it yourself by somebody with previous experience, and you will need to have practised the technique yourself on a child or colleague before trying to disseminate the method further. Actually tackling the tasks that the tutors and tutees will be addressing themselves to will give you extremely useful insight into the difficulties which they are going to face, and it will certainly not be time wasted. This does mean of course that time has to be found for relevant staff to attend training sessions, with all the implicit difficulties of covering for their classes meantime.

Participant training — organisation

It is essential that the initial launch of the project at the first training meeting goes well — your project must get off to a flying start rather than fall flat on its face. Training the children themselves individually or in pairs may be highly effective, but would be extremely time consuming and therefore not efficient, and most teachers opt to train the children in groups. Sometimes there are initial training meetings for the tutors and tutees as two separate groups, but in other circumstances tutors and tutees are trained together from the outset. If you have initial meetings for tutors and tutees separately, perhaps for an initial general orientation, remember that specific training meetings must always lead on immediately to direct practice of the techniques to be utilised, so you will need to get tutors and tutees together before too long. If in doubt, get them together earlier rather than later.

50

Venue and space

You will need to specify well in advance the date, time and place of your training sessions. The number of training sessions, their length and frequency will also need to be made clear to all concerned. This allows the tutors and tutees to look forward to their experience and (perhaps) become excited about the impending novel event. It also allows you to make very sure that colleagues are not going to claim the space you intend to use for practice for a last minute play rehearsal or TV programme.

The physical space in which training is going to occur will probably need the facility for all the participants to sit in a large group and listen to a talk and watch a demonstration, but there will also be a need for chairs (and possibly tables) to be available for subsequent practice, if this is to be incorporated in the same session. Thus, plenty of seats need to be available and their mobility to fulfil two purposes should be considered. Particularly with oral reading projects, remember that noise levels can be a problem, especially in the early stages of training when tutors and tutees will not have learnt to modulate their volume.

Materials and equipment

If audio-visual equipment (e.g. video) is to be used during the training session, try to ensure that you are prepared for Murphy's law to strike at the least opportune moment. The requisite equipment must be: not in use elsewhere, transportable to the location of the training, in good working order and compatible with basic services in the training space. Nothing is more distracting or disruptive to efficient learning than having, for example, to wait for an increasingly hysterical teacher to change the bulb in an overhead projector.

The materials to be used for the training session will also need to be readily and reliably available. You may choose to have available for scrutiny the whole range of possible materials, but for the actual practice it will be much better if the specific items and tasks for use by each pair during the practice session have been pre-selected, thus avoiding much meandering while hunting for an appropriate item. Even in projects where the tutors or tutees are in general to be given a fairly free choice of materials and tasks, paradoxically the training meeting may be the one occasion where you need to control the difficulty level of the materials more rigidly. If, for example, you are using the Paired Reading technique, tutor/tutee practice of the Reading Together aspect makes little sense if the tutee has chosen a very easy book which he or she is quite capable of reading independently.

Participant training — content

Verbal and written instruction

Some teachers tend to over-estimate the impact talking *to* children (lecturing) has upon subsequent behaviour, and this tends to be particularly true of teachers who are used to working with older age groups. Equally, teachers often over-estimate the ease with which children can assimilate information reliably from written materials. In fact, direct verbal instruction and written instruction (in pamphlets or lists of 'dos and don'ts') cannot be assumed to be effective training methods on their own, although they form essential components of any training procedure. Certainly a verbal explanation of the overall structure and purposes of the project will be given by way of introduction, followed by further detailed explanation of the materials and techniques to be used. But keep it brief! Many children, particularly those with any learning difficulty, will be 'switching off' after ten minutes of listening, if not earlier. Take care that the vocabulary you use in your verbal instruction is simple, and that any more unusual words you use are carefully defined for the children. This issue commonly arises in relation to the use of the words 'tutor' and 'tutee', which some project co-ordinators working with young children prefer to substitute with words like 'helper'. In actual fact, providing care is taken to define the meaning of the words in advance, their use with even young children can help to give the exercise an air of novelty and heighten its status.

Written instruction may take the form of continuous prose in a pamphlet, but again problems of assimilation of continuous information may arise for some children. Obviously the readability of the pamphlet should be kept as low as possible, since it is desirable that both tutor and tutee are able to refer to it subsequently to check anything of which they may be unsure. However, it may be much more useful to use various forms of checklist, flow chart, diagram, picture or cartoon, and so on. For essential reminders about the most important 'rules', posters or individual 'cue cards' may be helpful. It is worth remembering the old adage from industry that nobody reads anything which cannot be contained on one side of a piece of paper.

Demonstration

Having provided verbal and written instruction, it may be worthwhile allowing some time for questions and discussion. However, many of the questions and confusions arising could probably more readily be dealt with by proceeding very rapidly to a demonstration of the required behaviour. This demonstration could be a videotape available as a standard package from a support agency, or (more convincingly) one made in school. However, there is no need for such sophisticated technology, since it is equally possible for the teacher to demonstrate how to use the technique and materials, either with a willing and confident intending or previous tutee, or with another teacher playing the role of tutee. Once a first successful project has been run, experienced tutors and tutees can be brought back to demonstrate for subsequent groups of children embarking on the same experience, and this kind of demonstration tends to have the most impact of all.

Guided practice and feedback

Immediate practice of the tutoring technique is then esential, and feedback should be given from the professionals as soon as possible. In some projects, tutors practice the tutoring technique by role play on each other before being exposed to the tutees, and this may be a useful form of organisation if the tutoring technique is particularly complex. In many cases however, it should be possible to proceed directly to practice in the intended tutor/tutee pairs. In the 'reciprocating teacher model', the transfer of tutor role from the teacher to the intended tutor is a gradual process developed through steadily increasing amounts of practice in a large group situation.

Checking and remediation

The behaviour of the tutorial pairs needs close monitoring during the practice session, and this can put a considerable strain on staffing resources. In a practice session of 20 to 30 minutes, a professional cannot expect to observe in detail the tutoring technique of more than five or six pairs. Thus if large groups are being trained, a substantial number of 'mastery checkers' who are conversant with the techniques and materials will need to be available — this is undoubtedly the most labour-intensive part of the training procedure. Those pairs who demonstrate that they have learned the procedures rapidly can be praised and left to continue, but those pairs who are struggling or using deviant technique will need immediate extra individual tuition until they have fully mastered the procedures. Typically, each mastery checker is likely to find that two of the six pairs they are monitoring have learnt the technique extremely well and merely require social reinforcement, another two will have the technique more or less

53

right albeit rather shakily, but are thought to be likely to improve with a little practice, while a further two will be doing something completely aberrant, and may need to be helped individually through considerable unlearning before a virtual re-teaching of the technique from scratch can occur. Much time will be spent with these last two pairs.

Organisation and contracting

Once the children have been brought to mastery on techniques and materials, they will need briefing about the organisational 'nuts and bolts' of the day to day running of the project. This will include details about access to materials, means of record keeping, arranging times and places for tutorial contact, and the procedures for further help and follow up (some of these are dealt with in greater detail below). A brief written reminder of these organisational details may be helpful.

Some teachers choose to establish 'contracts' between tutors and tutees, or between project co-ordinators and tutors and tutees. Some emphasis can be placed on the voluntary nature of the project, with frequent reference to the undesirability of dropout, together with a little preaching about the significance of the decision to participate. Tutors and tutees should decide consciously to be either *in* the project or *out* of it, and it should be made clear that half measures will not be acceptable (especially by the peer group). In some projects, co-ordinators have made the two- or three-way contract written, with copies being held by all parties, in order to add to the solemn grown-up nature of the project. Of course, if a participant actually has to be berated by reference to the written contract, it may well be a sign that their motivation is any event so low that their continuing inclusion in the project is probably a waste of time. Efforts to retain unwilling tutors or tutees in the project should therefore not be too strenuous, but the project co-ordinator should perhaps make a conscious decision about the extent to which any withdrawal should become public knowledge. If the motivation of other participants is in a fragile state, one 'escapee' could start a fashion. On the other hand, if the motivation of the other participants remains very strong, the odd one out who withdraws from the project may be subject to considerable approbation from the peer group.

MONITORING

During the course of the project, it is important that the co-ordinating teacher keeps a close eye on how things are going, in order to be able to nip any incipient problems in the bud, to dispense plentiful praise and enthusiasm to keep motivation high, to ensure that technique does not show signs of 'drift', to check that the tutorial pairs or groups are maintaining positive social relationships, to be sure that materials are being used in an appropriate sequence or with reference to relevant levels of difficulty, and generally to keep themselves fully informed about the complexity and richness of the learning which should be taking place. Especially in a first project, close monitoring will be essential to ensure that the maximum benefit is gained by all participants.

Self-referral

In the spirit of co-operation which permeates peer tutoring, the children themselves may be the first to report difficulty or seek help. At a minor level, in a reading project such self-referral may revolve around the pair asking the meaning of words which are unfamiliar to both tutor and tutee, but children should also be encouraged to report readily difficulties in accommodating to each other's habits without feeling that they are 'telling tales'.

Both tutor and tutee should be clear about to whom they can self-refer, and this of course has implications for the regular availability of 'expert' help. The advantages of an age-peer project within one class are again considerable in this respect. It is also helpful to give the participants a clear notion of the nature and size of problems which they should self-refer, together with some examples. If a participant who is known to be of high status in the peer group can be prompted to be the first to refer a fairly minor problem, the other children will soon follow suit. In an oral reading project, it may be possible to designate a spare or back-up tutor as 'word-finder', who circulates with a dictionary to help out pairs who have failed to understand a particular word. In some projects, a record is kept of problems arising in order that they may be discussed with all the project participants as a group at a later time.

Self-recording

Some form of recording of tasks completed, books read, etc., during the project is highly desirable. This forms a tangible demonstration of achievement and progress for the children, and is of considerable interest for the supervising teacher. It is entirely logical that these records should be kept by the children themselves. With more wide-ranging tutoring materials, simple diaries can be kept by each pair, while projects utilising much more specific materials will generate much more precise records (e.g. within the precision teaching framework).

If the record keeping can be shared by tutor and tutee, then so much the better. In some projects the tutee records basic details such as date, materials completed and so on, while the tutor records some words of praise or other comment. Even quite young children prove to be surprisingly good at writing positive comments about their tutees, and learning to both give and receive praise without embarrassment is a valuable component of peer tutor projects. By and large, tutor comments should be as positive as possible, with any problems discussed directly with the project co-ordinator via self-referral.

In some cases the tutors begin to run out of imagination with respect to their positive comments, and this is an experience which has been shared by teachers who have had to write scores of end-of-year reports. The vocabulary of praise used by tutors can extend much further into the vernacular than a teacher would countenance for themselves, and ideas for praise words can be supplied by the tutee or the comments negotiated between tutor and tutee, although written down by the tutor. Dictionaries of praise can be made.

The records themselves should be checked each week by the supervising teacher, who can also record some favourable comment and add an official signature, perhaps together with other signs of approval such as house points or merit marks for a particularly meritorious week's work. The participants will however need to be clear about who is going to check the self-recording, when this is to occur, where the records are to be delivered to, and how frequently this is to be done.

Discussion

Many projects feature review meetings between co-ordinating teachers and the tutors and tutees. These can occur with the tutors and tutees separately or together, and with them in groups or as individuals. The general aim is to discuss how the project is going in general, and any further specific problem occurring in particular pairs. Group sessions can be valuable for tutors and/or tutees to discover that other pairs are having the same problems as they are. On the other hand, individual meetings will elicit more feedback from quiet and shy individuals, but will be much more time consuming. The frequency, duration and nature of such review meetings vary greatly from project to project. Sometimes regular 'planning' or 'de-briefing' meetings have been held between tutors and co-ordinators. It is probably useful if everybody knows in advance when these are going to occur, but self-referral in the meantime must also be encouraged. In projects where tokens or other reinforcers are made available for tutee improvement, some co-ordinators call group meetings to review comparative progress in terms of token acquisition. This can serve to give the whole project a strongly competitive flavour, which could do much to damage seriously the promotion of co-operative learning. From a European perspective, even the calling of such meetings to announce the gaining of tangible reinforcers *by* the group as a whole *for* the group as a whole may seem to be an unnecessary artifice, except in very special situations.

Direct observation

Of all the monitoring procedures, direct observation is by far the most revealing. Where a supervising teacher is present during the tutoring, particularly with age-peer projects in class time, much can be gleaned by observing individual pairs in rotation. The peer tutoring session is not an opportunity for the teacher to 'get on with some marking'. On the contrary, the teacher should either be setting a good example by themselves working with project materials or with a surplus tutee, or (more usefully) they should be circulating round the group observing and guiding children as necessary. In addition, it is possible to ask a particularly expert child tutor who is not otherwise engaged to act as an observer in a similar way and report back to the teacher. A simple checklist of the elements of the technique or other procedure may be useful to help to structure the observations of the 'monitors'. This could be very similar to, although perhaps a little more elaborate than, the checklist of 'rules' which could have been given to the tutorial pairs as part of the initial training procedure. It is also possible to use video or audio recording for monitoring purposes, and this can be very useful for feedback to individual pairs or the group as a whole, as well as being valuable as a training aid for subsequent projects. However it does take a little time and expertise to arrange.

Project process

Some form of check on basic organisational parameters of the project will also be necessary. The attendance of tutors and tutees at scheduled contact times will particularly require monitoring. You may find, for instance, that tutoring sessions scheduled for the very beginning of the school day are affected by irregularities in public transport, while those which are scheduled for the end of the school day or after school may be rendered problematic at certain times of the year by inclement weather or dark nights. There may be other spontaneous events or acts of God which interfere with the physical space available for tutoring, or create many distractions to it. If review meetings are to be held between tutorial participants and project co-ordinators, attendance at these and response in them needs to be checked. The availability of appropriate materials will require constant monitoring, as will the frequency and nature of selection and use of these. Organisational problems must be nipped in the bud at the earliest possible moment, and adjustments or modifications introduced as soon as possible.

EVALUATION

Some form of evaluation will certainly be a feature of your project, even if it is only based on subjective perceptions and general observations. If you hope to evaluate in a way which gives results of any consistency, reliability or validity, your planning at the outset will need to cover this area. To wait until the end of the project before attempting to evaluate its success is a recipe for confusion and self-deception, and all you will be able to check on a *post-hoc* basis is whether the 'consumers' say they were satisfied, and whether they have more or less positive attitudes towards their experiences. While this kind of 'evaluation' can give the project organiser a nice warm rosy glow, the 'grateful testimonials' approach will be regarded with cynicism by many hard-headed professionals. Having said that, to evaluate thoroughly can be fairly time consuming, and there is no point in devoting scarce time to this part of the exercise unless you have particular objectives in mind.

Positive evaluation information can be extremely valuable to feed back in suitable form to the tutoring participants to enhance even further their motivation. It may also be useful for a wide range of social, educational and quasi-political purposes. Evaluation information can be useful in a host of ways in addition to its primary purpose, which is to check whether what you have done has worked, in order to enable you to adjust or improve your organisation on a subsequent occasion. Positive evaluation results can serve to improve the project co-ordinator's motivation, but if in the final analysis there is no clear purpose in mind, then don't do it, for it is likely to be a waste of time.

The basic principles of designing an evaluation procedure are covered in greater detail later (Chapter 7), but some of the main considerations will briefly be reviewed here.

Firstly, a consideration of the research design is necessary. Most adequate evaluation will include at least a 'before and after' assessment of some sort, hence the need for planning to be built in from the outset. The school may already routinely collect data in the curriculum area in question, and thus information on progress prior to peer tutoring and after peer tutoring could be readily available. Wherever possible, it is useful to establish a control or comparison group of children who are not experiencing peer tutoring, or are having some alternative 'dummy' experience which includes as much time on the curriculum task and individual attention as the main project.

In measuring attainment gains, decisions have to be taken about whether to use some form of norm-referenced testing (to compare progress with normal expectations) or to use some form of criterion-referenced testing (which would check mastery of specific knowledge or information and tasks and skills learned). The latter approach tends to give bigger gains *per se*, because the assessment is more closely related to what has been tutored, but the former gives a better index of generalisation to other materials. Some form of qualitative analysis could be applied including error frequency counts, increased speed, etc., and of course the precision teaching format automatically generates results of this kind. For either a norm- or criterion-referenced approach, a decision will have to be made about whether to assess individually or in a group — this is basically a choice between the quick and easy but unreliable as against the slow and time consuming but more detailed and trustworthy approach.

The social gains which can accrue from tutoring will probably be evident from direct observation, but attempts could be made to measure this in other ways, referring to either improved relationships or improved behaviour or both. Unfortunately the paper and pencil measures employed (most typically checklists, rating scales, sociometry and so forth) tend to be of low reliability. Number of disciplinary referrals can be counted, but again these tend to be of doubtful reliability. Attitudinal data tends to be equally nebulous. This can come from individual or group interview or discussion, which could be tape recorded for later analysis, or from a variety of question-naires, ratings or checklists. It will be obvious that attitudinal and social gains should be the subject of assessment in both tutors and tutees, and separate devices may be necessary for this exercise for the two groups, but remember that attainment and cognitive gains should also be checked in both groups, since the tutors may be expected to gain as much if not more than the tutees in these areas too.

As previously mentioned, the collection of 'process' data about the organisational effectiveness of the project is essential. You will need to know if the training was carried out satisfactorily, if planning and review meetings occurred on time and were attended well, if records and other self-report data has been collated and checked as intended (so it can be analysed and related to other outcomes), whether all materials were readily available and used, whether the techniques were used properly, whether tutorial relationships were positive, whether mastery was checked as required by the tutors, whether self-referral by either tutorial partner was frequent across all pairs, whether 'take-homes' went home regularly and tokens and points were dis-pensed consistently, and so on. Attendance rates, distribution of lengths of tutoring sessions, information from observational checklists, and so forth can all be analysed and related to 'product' or outcome information from testing.

Whatever your best efforts, you can be sure that there will be some surprises. Observation may indicate a variety of unpredicted side effects, both positive and negative. You will be interested to see generalisation from the tutoring sessions to other participants (who may begin tutoring spontaneously even though not part of the project) and to other times, other materials and other curriculum areas. Once you have this kind of motivation and enthusiasm beginning to bubble in the peer group, you will soon begin to think of ways of capitalising upon it. Peer tutoring does tend to generate contagious enthusiasm right through an establishment. Generalisation from the specific tutor-ing curriculum to other wider areas of school life may be evident — thus there may be evidence elsewhere of improved examination results, a higher percentage of academic assignment completion across the curriculum, and so forth.

At this stage, it is easy to be so persuaded by the positive impact of your efforts that you devote all your time to establishing new, grander and more wide ranging peer tutor projects. A word of caution is necessary. Many educational innovations have shown good short-term impact, but at longer term follow-up the positive results have been found to have 'washed out'. It is thus worth devoting a little of your precious time to both short- and long-term follow-up of social and attainment gains in your original project group. For the project to have been *really* worthwhile, some enduring effect should be perceptible six months later, twelve months later and perhaps two years later. How realistic it is to expect one short intervention to have an impact that remains discernible much longer than this is a matter for considerable debate among educational evaluators. In the long run, an accumulation of spontaneous and random events is likely to mask the impact of almost anything.

FEEDBACK

The monitoring and evaluation information will need collating and summarising in some way, or (to be more precise) in two ways. A very simple way of presenting the favourable results and information to the children themselves is necessary to encourage them and promote further growth of confidence. A more 'scientific' collation will be necessary to present to interested colleagues, particularly those who will try to pick holes in your write-up. The information for this latter exercise need not necessarily be any less simple, merely different in emphasis.

It is worth making clear from the outset who is to take responsibility for the collation of information in these various ways, otherwise it might lie around on scraps of paper in drawers forever. Decisions must be taken about how to summarise the data for the various purposes, what balance of verbal, numerical and graphic presentation to use, and whether to incorporate any analysis of statistical significance (and if so which).

Feedback to the children can be group or individual, with the tutors and tutees separate or together. Do not assume that the children will be easily fobbed off by some vague generalisations from 'Miss' or 'Sir'. They are likely to want something more tangible and structured than that. You must make a decision about whether individual pairs are given information about their own progress, bearing in mind that even if they are not given comparative information they will soon be asking their friends for this in the playground, or whether the group as a whole should merely be given information about improvement based on group averages.

As evaluation information is given to the participants, it is always useful to make the feedback process reciprocal, and encourage them to give you their views (verbally or in writing or both) on how the project went, and how it could be improved for another generation on a subsequent occasion. Very often the children will make suggestions which are contradictory, and therefore rather difficult to implement, but some of their suggestions will undoubtedly be insightful and extremely helpful when organising further projects.

At the end of the initial phase of the project, joint decisions have to be made about the future. At this point, the views of the children must be taken very much into account. Some may wish to continue peer tutoring with the same frequency, others may wish to continue but with lesser frequency, while a few may be wanting a complete rest at least for a while. When in doubt, a good rule of thumb is to go for the parsimonious option. It will be better to leave some of the children a little 'hungry' and have them pestering you to launch another project in six weeks time, rather than let peer tutoring meander on indefinitely until it quietly expires. At this point of decision-making, also beware of trying to cater for a wide variety of choices from different tutoring pairs. The organisation of the project could become unbelievably complicated if you attempted to accommodate the varying desires for continuation of large numbers of children. It is probably as well to stick with what the majority vote for. Peer tutoring can thus be seen to be not only co-operative but democratic as well.

It may prove equally difficult to identify a significant voting majority for any particular proposed change, whether it be in technique, materials, curriculum area or form of organisation. It will also be difficult to obtain a majority view on whether pairings should be changed. Nevertheless, such discussions are useful as an exercise in democracy, language development and organisational problem solving, even if it is the project co-ordinator who at the end of the day has to make the final (and possibly somewhat arbitrary) decision.

We have noted that a few projects have built in frequent token acquisition for small increments in skill, and that most projects have preferred to use the more naturalistic and readily available social reinforcement. However, you may feel it desirable for those tutors and tutees who have completed the initial phase of commitment of your project satisfactorily to receive some form of public commendation for their efforts. Some projects present the children with certificates of merit or effort, small tokens of esteem such as badges and pens, and so on. These can be presented in a public gathering in the school, but with older pupils public praise needs to be used carefully. It is always worth seeking the views of the participants on the nature of any final ceremonial. Needless to say, both tutors and tutees should be equally eligible for commendation. Some projects have chosen to count a peer tutoring experience for academic credit, perhaps including the tutor's efforts as part of some nominal community service curriculum. Quite apart from its value as reinforcement for the tutorial pairs, some form of public commendation is also useful publicity which may assist in the later recruitment of new tutors.

REASSURANCE

The danger with any form of instruction is of course that by breaking what is basically a naturally acquired skill into its constituent parts, it promotes the 'technicalisation' of something which is actually not that difficult. Right now you may well be feeling that the organising of peer tutoring is a great deal more difficult and complicated than you had first thought, and you may not be at all sure that you haven't gone off the idea.

Be reassured. Many of the potential problems mentioned above will never come to afflict you. Setting up your first peer tutor project will undoubtedly be a great deal easier than you imagined. What we have tried to do here is cover all of the possible points of decision. At many of these points, you can decide 'No', and proceed carefully to organise a very simple project, which will probably be very successful. In this case, your completion of the Structured Planning Guide (Chapter 5) will be very brief, and the guide will have many blank spaces sprinkled with 'No' or 'Not Applicable'.

However, if your project should happen to be less successful than you would have liked, you will be able very easily to review your decisions about organisation and determine where you might have gone wrong or left something out that might have been crucial. Thus, if you don't succeed first time, you will certainly succeed at the *second* attempt. Now at least you are prepared for anything. Well, *almost* anything.

5

Structured Planning Guide

This guide lists the major questions to ask and areas of decision to consider when planning a peer tutor project. You will see that they are laid out under ten main headings: Context, Participants, Curriculum, Materials, Contact, Technique, Training, Monitoring, Evaluation and Feedback.

Don't be put off by the apparent size of the guide. It list many options, only a few of which will be relevant to you. As you make your decisions, record them in writing. This will constitute a useful organisational summary to make further copies of for distribution to other interested parties.

The guide strives for a degree of generality which makes it applicable to all sorts of peer tutoring projects, hopefully without losing too much specificity and practicality. It will probably prove easier to use when establishing a true age-peer project within one class, or in some other group already in naturalistic contact. Projects like this are in any event easier to operate, and readers are advised to start with this kind of project. After gaining experience, a cross-age tutor project in one establishment could be tried, perhaps followed by a cross-school project. If you make all these work, you will no longer need this guide. Good luck!

A: The Context

(1) Problems specific to the situation
- to be addressed by the tutoring project?
- likely to impair the success of the project?
  (i)   low motivation in students?
  (ii) low standards of attainment?
  (iii) poor inter-group relationships?
  (iv) high incidence of behaviour problems?

    (v)   ethnic minorities, second language?

    (vi) inappropriate accommodation, curriculum, teaching methods?

    (vii) other?

(2) What supports are available?

    (i)   from colleagues in school

    (ii) from outside agencies and helpers

    (iii) who will stand in your way?

          — how will you get round this?

Verbal support	What practical help in time and resources will they contribute?

(3) Objectives of the tutoring project

    (specified in observable, operational terms)

       (i)

       (ii)

       (iii)

       (iv)

B: Selection and Matching of Participants

    Target Groups: Tutors:

                 Tutees:

(1) Background Factors — existing maturity, work habits, co-operative ethos, etc.

(2) Recruiting — how should recruiting be conducted?

                — in person, in writing, advertising, publicity, grapevine?

(3) Age — age-peer or cross-age tutors?

                — what are the pros/cons of the two options?

(4) Numbers — pairs or small groups (of what size?) to what total?

                how many can be effectively monitored?

(5) Ability   — range of ability in tutors and tutees?
— how to maintain a tutor/tutee differential neither too big nor too small?

(6) Relationships   — how to accommodate existing positive or negative relationships?
— how to accommodate weak and strong personalities?

(7) Participant Preference   — accept to what degree? What system for showing preference?
— mixed-sex or mixed-race pairings to be encouraged?

(8) Standby Tutors   — back-up/spare/supply tutors to cover absence/dropout?
— how many needed?

(9) Parental Agreement   — necessary? How much information to give? (See 'Handout for Parents' in Chapter 8.)

(10) Incentives   — material or other incentives for tutors? — or tutees?
— rely on intrinsic motivation?

C: Curriculum Area

(1) Reading — oral reading? word recognition? decoding? comprehension?

(2) Mathematics — drill or conceptual?

(3) Language — expressive and/or receptive?

(4) Spelling — words or skills?

(5) Writing — creative

(6) Writing — punctuation and grammar

(7) Thinking skills and problem solving

(8) Second languages

(9) Science

(10) Other

How will this conflict with the 'official' curriculum?

D: Materials

(1) Structure
— highly structured and sequenced or open-ended?
— who has time to prepare structured materials, or can existing packages be used?

(2) Difficulty
— finely graded and of controlled difficulty?
— or open choice with teaching of choosing skills?
(NB: difficulty ceiling controlled to *tutor's* level)

(3) Choosing
— tutor or tutee to choose, or by negotiation?
— open choice or open from a specific level?
— how much choosing *practice* before giving guidance?

(4) Availability
— what financial cost? Any chance of a loan?
— expensive hardware required? Cost of consumables?
— can tutorial pairs make materials?

(5) Sources
— in-house existing materials, library loan, special collection, import from other establishments, material from participants' homes?

(6) Access
— how frequent and easy is access to the materials?
— who takes the initiative on access, tutor or tutee or other?

(7) Progression
— who determines when to move onto other material, and how?

(8) Records
— what recording materials necessary, who completes, who owns, who replenishes stock?

E: Contact

(1) Time
— classtime/break time/both/after school?
— times fixed for all or various by negotiation?

(2) Place
— classroom/leisure or play area/other?
— check seating availability and acoustic absorbency (noise!)

(3) Duration
— 15, 20, 30, 45, 60 minutes?

(4) Frequency — 3, 4, 5, 10 times weekly?

(5) Project Period — 6, 8, 10 weeks, 1 term (semester), longer?

(6) Problems — in cross-age tutoring, how to match timetables?
— and how much disruption from student movement?

F: Technique

(1) Packaged Techniques — Reading Together, Paired Reading, Pause Prompt Praise, Programmed Tutoring, Companion Study, SWRL, etc.
— Predict, Question, Summarise, Clarify or SQ3R, Direct Instruction, Cued Spelling, etc.

(2) Precision Teaching — a useful review format, but how to actually *teach*?

(3) Behavioural Methods — contingencies for correct performance?
— what kinds of reinforcement?

(4) General Teaching Skills — presentation, explanation, demonstration, prompting, checking, feedback, deficit identification, remediation

(5) Drill — will tutor or tutee die of boredom first?

(6) Combinations — of the above

(7) Correction Procedure — must be simple and clearly defined

(8) Praise — specify frequency of, and circumstances for, praise.
— verbal and non-verbal, must be genuine!
— and how to avoid criticising!

(9) Social Components — establishing rapport, sharing interest, verbal and non-verbal social skills

(10) Trouble-Shooting — what do they do if they hit problems?

G: Training

(1) Staff Training — are all relevant professionals fully conversant with materials and techniques?

(2) Participant Training — Organisation

(i) Grouping	— individual or group?
	— tutors and tutees separately or together or both?
(ii) Venue	— date/time/place?
	— number/length of sessions?
(iii) Audio-visual Equipment	— available/working?
	— other teaching aids?
(iv) Materials for Tutoring	— available, pre-selected?
	— controlled for practice?
(v) Practice Space	— check seats/noise levels

(3) Participant Training — Content

(i) Verbal Instruction	— keep it brief!
(ii) Written Instruction	— pamphlets, checklists, flowcharts, reminders
(iii) Demonstration	— from teacher (role play) or experienced tutor or on video
(iv) Guided Practice and Feedback	— tutors and tutees directly, or by role play?
(v) Mastery Checking	— of individual pairs — how many checkers available?
(vi) Remedial Tuition	— for those in need — how many remediators available?
(vii) Organisation	— briefing about organisational issues, contact, records, etc.
(viii) Contracting	— in some/all cases?

H: Monitoring

(1) Self-referral	— by tutor or tutee — to whom?
	— how available is 'expert' help?
	— what sort/size of problems to be referred?
(2) Self-recording	— by tutor or tutee or both?
	— for every session or less frequently?
	— positive and negative aspects, or just positive?
	— what criteria and/or vocabulary?
	— checking records — who, when, where, how often?
(3) Discussion	— group or individual?
	— tutors and tutees separate or together?
	— frequency and duration of review meetings?

(4) Direct Observation
- by far the most revealing!
- checklist of criteria/desired behaviour to hand?
- by project coordinator or spare tutor or other?
- video or audio-tape for feedback purposes?

(5) Project Process
- what checks on organisational aspects?
- frequency/duration of review meetings between professionals?
- what adjustment/modifications are needed?

I: Evaluation

(1) Purpose of the Evaluation
- If there's no purpose, don't do it!

(2) Current Assessment Practice
- extend to give time series data? (i.e. pre-project gains c.f. project gains)

(3) Research Design
- pre-post/baseline/comparison group/etc?
- separate measures for tutors and tutees?

(4) Normative Testing
- standardised tests to compare with 'normal' expectation? — and perhaps check generalisation

(5) Criterion-Referenced Testing
- mastery testing to see if specific tasks/skills/information learnt — gives better results!
- error frequency counts, materials mastered, increased speed, etc?

(6) Individual vs Group Testing
- the quick and unreliable vs the slow but detailed

(7) Attitudinal Data
- from individual or group interview/discussion?
- from questionnaires, checklists, ratings?
- other observers' subjective reaction?

(8) Social Gains
- improved relations or behaviour?
- how to measure? Checklists, sociometry, disciplinary referrals?

(9) Self-report Data
- analyse and relate to other outcomes

(10) Other Process Data
- attendance, mean session length, observation checklists, etc.
- analyse and relate to other outcomes

(11) Spin-off
- observations of unpredicted side effects —

- positive *and* negative!
- generalisation to other participants, times, materials, subject areas, etc.
- generalisation to exam results, assignment completion, etc.

(12) Follow-up   — short- and long-term follow-up data *highly* desirable

J: Feedback

(1) Collation of Information
- who co-ordinates this?
- how variously for different consumers?

(2) Data Analysis
- how to summarise?
- what balance of verbal/numerical/graphic?
- analysis of statistical significance?

(3) Feedback to Participants
- group or individual?
- tutors/tutees separate or together?
- verbal/written audio-visual?

(4) Feedback from Participants
- group or individual?
- verbal or written?
- any suggestions for improvement?

(5) Further Contracting
- continue tutoring/stop/reduce frequency?
- changed technique?
- changed materials?
- changed subject area?
- changed pairings?
- changed organisation?

(6) Accolades
- tutors and/or tutees?
- public commendation?
- academic credit?
- certificates, badges, etc?

6

Effectiveness Research

Teachers tend to be very practical, which is good, but they also tend to be rather parochial, which is less good. Typically, teachers are more likely to implement a new method if they have seen it in action in a neighbouring school or if they have had good reports of it in person from somebody they know. The research literature is often regarded with a degree of suspicion, as being of doubtful relevance to life in the classroom.

While it is true that much of 'academic' research is indeed of doubtful relevance to life *anywhere*, let alone in the classroom, there is some effectiveness research which is of great pragmatic value, and discrimination of babies from bathwater is necessary. You will need to refer to the background literature to improve your own motivation to mount a peer tutoring project, and to reassure yourself that you have a high chance of success (given careful organisation). You will need to be able to refer to it to persuade colleagues, perhaps those in positions of authority, that what you propose is not just a crackpot idea of your own. Equally importantly, you will need to refer to research results when informing the parents of the children you intend to include in your project of the requirements and implications of the programme, or the parents may get some very strange ideas about what you are up to!

There is a considerable volume of good quality research literature on the subject of peer and cross-age tutoring, much of it originating from the United States. There is far too much for us to consider in detail here, and for practical purposes this will rarely be necessary. Thus, in the rest of this chapter, the primary concern will be with the conclusions of the more substantial *reviews* of research which have appeared since 1970. Additionally, some of the more recent individual research reports in specialist areas will be considered. Readers with a strong interest in peer tutoring in a particular curriculum area or with an esoteric client group should easily be able to trace back the requisite references, by consulting the reference lists in the review publications.

REVIEWS OF RESEARCH

As renewed interest in peer tutoring grew rapidly in the United States during the 1960s, an over-view of the new initiatives was formulated by Gartner, Kohler and Riessman. This was published in 1971 under the title *Children Teach Children*. This was soon followed by another substantial volume by Rosenbaum (1973). Review publications came thick and fast as the popularity of peer tutoring surged in North America in the mid-1970s. Klaus (1975) produced a substantial work on patterns of peer tutoring throughout the United States, while Wilkes (1975) provided a detailed annotated bibliography. (Both of these items are less than easy to acquire from outside the United States.) Also in 1975, Bloom produced a compilation volume on peer tutoring which included contributions from many distinguished workers in the field.

The first major review

In 1976 Eberwein *et al.* produced a further annotated bibliography on volunteer tutoring programmes, but by far the most significant event of the year was the publication of the very widely read *Children as Teachers*, edited by Vernon Allen.

In this book, Feldman, Devin-Sheehan and Allen offered the first review of research which conformed to generally accepted 'academic' standards. (A similar review was also published under Devin-Sheehan's name in the *Review of Educational Research* in the same year.) The authors noted that the evidence concerning the effectiveness of peer tutoring programmes in the schools had often consisted of anecdotal reports rather than rigorous data. Some well-controlled research had also been conducted, but this was often in the minority. It was noted that although students with a variety of handicaps and problems were themselves reported anecdotally to benefit from serving as tutors, fortunately the carefully controlled experiments tended to support this weaker evidence. A number of studies had found that low achievers in reading made significant gains in reading ability following their tutoring of younger children. While it was clear that tutoring reliably resulted in improved attainment in the tutees, the evidence that tutors benefited *socially* or in personality terms was more variable in outcome and was often based on less reliable measures. Furthermore, there was some question as to whether a tutor with problems who might benefit from being a tutor was actually the most beneficial kind of tutor so far as the tutee was concerned. The empirical evidence on this latter issue yielded conflicting results. A number of studies had noted positive effects accruing to both tutors and tutees when tutoring was provided by children who themselves had problems, but a number of other studies had found that the positive effects which accrued to the tutor were not reflected in benefits to the tutee. Feldman, Devin-Sheehan and Allen concluded that:

> The literature on tutor characteristics suggests quite convincingly that a very broad range of students may benefit from acting as tutor. Whether or not the tutee will improve more from being tutored by a particular type of tutor is an open question; the evidence is mixed at this time. The crucial factor may be the relative level of competence between the tutor and the tutee.

The authors also considered the research on sex pairings in peer tutoring. A predominant belief was that same-sex pairs facilitated tutoring, but there was little empirical support for such an assertion, as most studies on tutoring had employed same-sex pairs. In those studies which had used different-sex pairings, there was no indication that this was less effective than same-sex pairings, although most subjects preferred to tutor a same-sex, rather than a different-sex, tutee. There was some evidence that in sibling peer tutor pairings, the most effective match was an older sister teaching a younger brother. There was some evidence that the experience of opposite-sex tutoring could lead to changes in preference for members of the opposite sex. Irrespective of sex pairing, one or two studies had noted that male tutees tended to benefit from peer tutoring more than female tutees.

Although much of the literature on tutoring used white, middle-class children as subjects, it was clear from a number of other studies that other racial and social class groupings produced significant academic improvement when tutoring children of the same race and status. Cross-race tutoring had been found to promote inter-racial interaction in one study, but not in another. There was some evidence that white, middle-class peer tutors were more likely to use positive reinforcement than black, middle-class tutors or lower-class tutors of either race. Interestingly, one study noted an increase in level of 'aspiration' following a year's experience of being a tutor — tutors from lower socio-economic levels began to aspire to occupations associated with upward social mobility.

Age differentials between tutors and tutees had varied widely in several studies, but there was little systematic evidence on the optimum age difference. What evidence was available suggested that a greater age difference between tutor and tutee resulted in rather better tutee performance, but on the other hand the nature of the interaction might be found more pleasant when the age range between tutor and tutee was closer.

It was noted that the vast majority of tutoring programmes consisted of one tutor paired with one tutee; few studies had examined the effect of tutoring in larger groups. What evidence was available was mixed, some evidence suggesting that one-to-one tutoring was more effective than tutoring in a group of three for at least some subjects (reading), for at least some ages (high school pupils), at least in the short run. Rather surprisingly, the effect of length of tutoring programme had also been under-researched. The assumption that the longer the tutoring programme, the more positive the cumulative effects would be, had little empirical support. However, there was evidence that one-to-one tutoring was of greater benefit than an equal amount of instructional time spent in an ordinary classroom situation.

Evidence on the effectiveness of training of tutors was also reviewed. Various studies had demonstrated the effects of training in terms of subsequently changed tutor behaviour. At that time, it was felt that the available research did not indicate unequivocally that any one particular method of training was superior to any other, and indeed there was surprisingly little data showing that training of tutors *per se* had a beneficial effect on tutoring. One study noted that tutors who did not expect an external reward exhibited a more positive emotional tone during tutoring and were more effective teachers than those tutors who had expected to be paid, implying that intrinsic motivation of tutors may be an important factor in determining the success of the experience.

Feldman *et al.* noted many problems of research methodology in the peer tutoring studies. For example, control groups were frequently conspicuous by their absence and many studies used a 'comparison group' of students who had not wished to volunteer for tutoring — hardly a reliable and valid comparison. In many studies the total amount of instructional time was not controlled, so the extent to which peer tutoring merely gave more practice remained a factor of unknown significance. The effects of novelty and special attention from adults and teachers had never been the subject of satisfactory control. Feldman *et al*. concluded:

> Unless investigators in this area make a stronger attempt to draw more directly upon the mainstream of psychological and educational theory, it is likely the research on tutoring will be rather fragmented, inconclusive and non-cumulative.

The United Kingdom perspective

Towards the end of the 1970s, peer tutoring had begun to attract attention in the United Kingdom, and Goodlad's *Learning by Teaching* was undoubtedly the first major British work on the subject. Goodlad devotes his Chapter 4 to a review of effectiveness research, but this is coloured by his own preference for 'softer' styles of evaluation. He justifies this thus: 'One might also state as an axiom that the more complex the tutoring experiment is (in its responsiveness to social needs), the less amenable it is to . . . research'.

Goodlad recommends that anyone organising a tutoring scheme should provide for some sort of evaluation, but notes that there is a tension between action and research. It is noted that volunteers can be highly motivated to succeed, and therefore bring with them their own Hawthorne Effect. For research purposes, it is usually desirable to hold tutoring time constant, keep tutor groups and control groups apart to minimise 'contamination', and maintain tutoring conditions constant or to vary them systematically, all of which rule out implementing *ad hoc* improvements indicated by experience. Goodlad feels that the anecdotal evidence ('positive testimony') as to the value of tutoring in improving the attitudes of tutors is enormous, and 'it is remarkable how unsuccessful "hard-nosed" research has been in supporting this'.

Turning to reviewing studies more systematically, Goodlad cites nine studies which had unequivocally demonstrated that *tutors* made cognitive gains as a result of their experiences. Affective outcomes had been more difficult to measure systematically. Some studies had shown that tutoring improved the self-concept of the tutor, while others had failed to do so. However, only one study reported systematic differences in classroom behaviour between tutors and control groups. The evidence for cognitive gains in the *tutees* was overwhelming, particularly with reference to reading skills. The most consistent reporting of cognitive gains for tutees (particularly in reading) came from the proponents of 'structured' tutoring. The mathematics area, too, had been well-researched. Tutees also showed affective gains, with some studies (at least) showing improved self-concept and one or two studies demonstrating improved behaviour.

Goodlad's review of factors which appeared significant in the effectiveness of tutoring largely confirms the previous findings of Feldman *et al.* (1976). It was additionally suggested that a greater age and experience gap between tutors and tutees was likely to be necessary if the material to be taught was more complex. However, even with complex subjects, an age/experience gap of three years would probably be quite adequate. There was some evidence that more frequent tutoring sessions were more effective than less frequent tutoring sessions over similar project periods. However, tutoring schemes had been effective over periods ranging from two weeks to two years.

There was little evidence on the issue of optimal length of tutoring session, which presumably would be highly variable according to the curriculum content and age of tutees. While one-to-three tutoring had been demonstrated to be as effective as one-to-one tutoring in some circumstances, the cost-effectiveness of the small group arrangement had to be balanced against the evident satisfaction which tutors and tutees derived from developing personal relationships with each other.

Training tutors generally improved their effectiveness, although the kind and complexity of training given to tutors had been highly various in different projects. Structured tutoring involving programmed instructional materials which allow the interaction between tutor and tutee to focus on specific, detailed tasks appeared best to serve the educational interests of the tutees. It is noted that while participants in tutoring schemes involving unstructured training may have favourable impressions of the effectiveness of what they are doing, this tends not to be supported by objective evidence. Finally, Goodlad noted that the introduction of structure into tutor training and curriculum materials was by no means incompatible with the derivation of personal satisfaction and improvements in self-concept by both participants. In fact structure and organisation were likely to promote these latter.

The biggest review

The beginning of the 1980s saw the release of another major book by Ehly and Larsen (1980). However, the largest and the most thorough academic research review of this period was undoubtedly that of Sharpley and Sharpley (1981), which deserves to be more widely known. These authors scrutinised reports on 82 peer tutor programmes, categorising them according to the characteristics of the participants, the tutoring process and the adequacy of research designs. Many of the reports were doctoral dissertations or unpublished papers which were not readily available.

On the question of impact of personal characteristics of tutor and tutee, the reviewers concluded that a very broad range of students could benefit from the tutoring experience. Low achievers in reading, poorly motivated students, and high achieving students had been able to benefit either academically, socially or cognitively from participation in tutoring programmes as either a tutor or a tutee. Detailed evidence on the question of whether or not a tutee would benefit more from being tutored by a particular type of tutor was not yet available. A few studies had manipulated tutor achievement level systematically, and the bulk of these reported that the achievement level of the tutors seemed unrelated to tutee achievement. The *relative* competence between the tutor and tutee could be of greater significance, irrespective of the ability of the tutor as compared to age norms. In some studies, high achieving tutors had shown no gains from their experience, while in some projects using low achieving tutors the tutees had failed to gain from the experience.

On the issue of sex-pairing, further evidence had accumulated that children tended to prefer a partner of the same sex, but there was no evidence that mixed-sex matching reduced cognitive gains. The tendency for male tutees to benefit more from tutoring than female tutees was increasingly evident. There was some evidence that female tutors tended to produce better gains in tutees than male tutors.

The issue of age differential between tutor and tutee had also been subjected to study. The age difference had ranged from adults tutoring pre-schoolers to same-age pairings, via every possible combination. Although one or two studies had found correlations between cognitive gains in tutees and the size of tutor-tutee age differential, the majority of the research had found no difference on this basis. Sharpley and Sharpley conclude that same-age tutors are as effective as disparate-age tutors in inducing cognitive advances in the tutees, but also that same-age tutors are more likely themselves to derive cognitive benefits as a result of their tutoring experiences. Systematic research on racial and socio-economic factors associated with tutoring remained sparse, with inconclusive or conflicting findings prohibiting any generalisations about the relationship of race and socio-economic status to tutoring outcomes.

So far as the optimum length of tutoring programme was concerned, conflicting theories abounded. Some workers favoured longer tutoring programmes on the assumption that they generated more positive effects, while others felt that tutor and tutee may become bored during lengthy projects. The reviewers note that positive effects had been reported from programmes which had run for as short a time as five days, and academic gains had been evident even from single session tutoring studies. Frequencies of tutoring had ranged from ten minutes to 60 minutes a session, and from one session per week to five sessions per week. The median number of sessions per week was slightly above three, and the median time slightly above 30 minutes. All of these studies had reported academic or social benefits with less than four hours tutoring per week. However, other studies with less than four hours tutoring per week had reported minimal gains, while *all* studies which had incorporated more than four hours per week had reported significant gains. Evidence on the relative impact of number of tutees per tutor remained sparse and conflicting.

Reading was certainly the most frequently mentioned task in the peer tutoring literature, but a number of other tasks and activities had been used in tutoring programmes with varying degrees of success. These included 16 studies focused on mathematics, two on spelling and two on language skills. Other curriculum areas included: social science, French and German languages, Spanish language, syntax, abstract cognitive skills, written expression, sorting games, conservation of number, associative responding, Piagetian structures, English, writing assignments, creative thinking, problem solving, writing a research paper, and drugs, sexuality and birth control.

The nature of the interaction within the tutoring situation had also been the subject of considerable study. Where tutors are merely required to provide feedback, they are likely to be less effective than where they actively involve themselves with the materials. There is some evidence that older tutors tend to be more demanding of tutees and more likely to depend on verbal interaction, while younger tutors interact in a more direct and pragmatic manner. Some workers had deployed token or tangible reinforcement within peer tutoring projects, in addition to the commonly emphasised social and affective reinforcement. Three experimental studies found no evidence that extrinsic reinforcement produced gains which were superior to non-reinforced groups, while another three studies claimed to have demonstrated that tangible reinforcement did improve the functioning of the tutees, at least on fairly simple tasks in the short term. The reviewers note: 'It is difficult to reconcile the conflicting results or to draw confident conclusions about reinforcement in the tutoring situation.'

In discussion of the impact of training on the tutoring process, a problem is the moveable definition of 'training'. A wide variation in the time allocated to tutor training and the methods used is evident. Variants of training used included: ten minutes training prior to each tutoring session; lessons taught to tutors before tutoring sessions; one hour's training per week; one training session before each of four tutoring sessions; a ten session training module as part of the tutors' own school curriculum.

In some studies, intensive pre-service training was followed by in-service training. A few studies had compared the effectiveness of trained versus untrained tutors in terms of techniques used or tutee achievement. Four studies suggested that tutor training produced positive results in tutor behaviour or tutee achievement, while only one study had found no difference. The results of studies of unstructured programmes and programmes utilising untrained tutors were very various. It seems that although unstructured programmes using untrained tutors can succeed, they are likely to have a lower success rate.

However, the question of what constitutes 'training' remains important. Some training has attempted to raise the frequency of 'teacher-like' behaviour in tutors (e.g. praising, demonstrating, etc.), while other training has focused much more specifically on the presentation of curriculum material associated with the programme. There was some evidence suggesting that training *per se* has a beneficial effect on tutors, irrespective of its focus. Presumably any form of apparently coherent training may have the effect of raising the confidence of the tutors. There was not at that stage any unequivocal evidence that any one method of training tutors was superior to any other.

Sharpley and Sharpley (1981) note that there are limitations in the research designs of many studies in terms of sampling, adequacy of criteria, measures, control groups and duration and intensity of intervention. Sample size and representativeness was often a problem, and many small or atypical samples could provide no basis for generalisation. An interesting feature was the absence of reporting of deleterious effects on tutors or tutees; these effects had either not been present or had not been reported. According to the authors, the literature review 'highlights the promise of peer teaching as a viable, low-cost means of individualising instruction'.

Sharpley and Sharpley provide an excellent set of tables summarising the outcomes of the 82 studies they reviewed. Those writing theses on peer tutoring should not fail to acquire a copy of these for reference. For our purposes, it is worth noting from their Table 3 that the text of their review gives great emphasis to those studies which have reported statistically significant findings. In terms of academic outcomes for tutors, 21 studies reported positive effects, none reported negative effects, but 29 reported non-significant effects. With reference to self-concept outcomes for tutors, five studies reported positive effects, no studies reported negative effects, but 18 studies reported non-significant effects. For academic outcomes for tutees, 35 studies reported positive effects, no studies reported negative effects, but 27 reported non-significant effects. For self-concept outcomes for tutees, three studies reported positive effects, no studies reported negative effects, and 18 studies reported non-significant effects. Thus, it is clear that a great many studies which are not often referred to have actually failed to demonstrate significant effects accruing from peer tutoring. Those mounting peer tutor projects should thus be cautious in their predictions, and not raise expectations of automatic success too high. It is perhaps worth bearing in mind however, that the Sharpley and Sharpley review included many unpublished dissertation studies, which are well known to be less likely to report significant results than studies which are published in journals. Nevertheless, it may well be that a practising teacher hoping to run a project will have even less time and perhaps no more expertise than the average Master's student, so take care!

A behaviourist viewpoint

A more subjective review was offered contemporaneously by Gerber and Kauffman in *The Utilisation of Classroom Peers as Behavior Change Agents* (1981), a book edited by Phillip Strain. The authors note that several studies have attempted to compare the effectiveness of peer tutoring to either teacher-led instruction or some form of self-instruction. In general, the results indicated that peer tutoring could be at least as effective as teacher-led instruction under certain conditions, and that tutoring as a supplement to teaching is likely to be better than teaching alone. However, they caution that the peer tutor is not a *free* resource. The use of peers as tutors simply represents a different allocation of the existing scarce resource of teacher time which may or may not result in greater productivity (cost-effectiveness).

It is noted that many studies fail to report in detail the amount of instructional resources required for training or maintaining the peer tutors in their task.

The Gerber and Kauffman review is set firmly within the tradition of behavioural psychology. There is considerable discussion of the extent to which making available group rewards for group improvement 'spontaneously' elicits peer tutoring behaviours in the children. Further than this, considerable emphasis is placed on 'programmed instructional material and an adequate reward structure'. Given this, it is claimed that the tutor can assist the tutee in 'transferring the learned behaviour to new settings once the tutor is established as the source of reinforcement for certain target behaviours'. Practising teachers may have some difficulty relating the behaviourist vocabulary of this review to everyday classroom practice. Reported work on the tendency for tutors of originally non-preferred tutees to respond more positively to the tutees as their performance improves as a result of tutor effort is useful, however. The authors conclude 'the findings suggest that peer tutoring may play a significant, even powerful, part in an overall instructional technology'. These authors feel that control of contingency arrangements should be given precedence in future research, but findings of past research would not seem to support this, as for many tutor-tutee pairs tutoring proves to be adequately intrinsically self-reinforcing.

The meta-analytic approach

A further review from yet another theoretical viewpoint is offered by Cohen et al. (1982). They utilised the 'meta-analysis' procedure which has become increasingly popular in the 1980s. Instead of the subjective evaluation of the traditional literature review, which remained subjective however much it tried to be systematic and conform to standard academic practice, 'meta-analysis' attempted a purely quantitative synthesis of disparate research findings. The computer-based search yielded a total of more than 500 titles relating to tutoring. However, once studies which lacked a full reportage of quantitative outcomes in both the tutored and the non-tutored control group were excluded, together with those studies which had major methodological flaws, only 65 studies remained. Unfortunately, the authors never make it clear how many of these studies involve children tutoring children, and how many involve the deployment of adult tutors. In 45 of 52 studies, tutored students out-performed control students, while in six studies control students did better and in one study there was no difference. The average effect size in the 52 studies was 0.40, a magnitude which can only be described as modest. However, some studies reported very large effect sizes. Studies which involved tutor training tended to produce larger effect sizes. Studies involving cross-age tutoring tended to produce larger effect sizes. Studies involving structured tutoring tended to produce larger effect sizes. Short-term projects tended to produce larger effect sizes. Larger effect sizes were produced in tutoring programmes in the mathematics area than in any other curriculum area. Tutees of low ability tended to generate larger effect sizes than tutees of middling ability. Effects tended to be larger on locally developed tests and smaller on nationally standardised tests. As is usual, studies described in dissertations reported smaller effects than did studies described in journal articles.

Eight studies reported results on student attitudes, and in all eight student attitudes were more positive in classrooms with tutoring programmes, although in only one case was this effect large enough to be considered statistically reliable. Nevertheless, results were consistent enough to sustain the conclusion that tutoring programmes had a positive effect on the tutees' attitudes towards the material being taught. Nine studies reported effects on tutee self-concept. In seven cases these favoured students in tutoring programmes, in two cases results favoured the control group. However, the average effect size was very small and not large enough to be considered statistically reliable.

Of the studies analysed, 38 examined achievement effects on tutors. In 33 studies, students who served as tutors performed better than control students in the relevant curriculum area. Results favoured control groups in the other five studies. Effect sizes for tutor gains tended to be even smaller overall. Five studies investigated *tutor* attitude towards tutoring subject matter, four studies indicating more positive attitudes among tutors than controls and one study the converse. The effects of tutoring programmes on self-concept of tutors were reported in 16 studies. In 12 studies the self-concept score of tutors was higher than for controls, and in the remaining four studies the converse was true. The average effect size for tutor self-concept was, however, small and of doubtful statistical reliability.

Overall, Cohen *et al.* (1982) conclude: 'These programmes have definite and positive effects on the academic performance and attitudes of those who receive tutoring. Tutoring programmes also have positive effects on children who serve as tutors, in attitudes and understanding. However, 'tutoring programmes have much smaller effects on the self-concept of children', despite the 'anecdotal reports of dramatic changes' in the literature.

Cohen *et al.* conclude that the results of their meta-analysis agree to a large extent with the conclusions of the more subjective, traditional literature reviews. There seems to be remarkable consistency in the findings of positive effects from peer tutoring in all the reviews studied.

RECENT RESEARCH

In the 1980s, interest in peer tutoring from researchers has not shown the sharp acceleration which characterised the 1970s, but work has continued at a steady pace in North America and interesting work has begun to emerge from other corners of the globe. It will only be possible here to mention briefly some of the more significant recent research, with particular emphasis being given to projects significant for the breadth and scale of application, or for their addressing of new curriculum areas, or for working with particularly difficult client groups.

It is now routinely demonstrated that peer tutors can be as effective as resource teachers in raising the academic attainments of handicapped students (e.g. Russell and Ford 1983). Structured tutoring systems have become increasingly popular, since as von Harrison (1976) noted, they combine structure with a highly sensitive and personal learning environment. This author's work on the structured tutoring of reading and mathematics has continued to develop over the years, and the costings cited are impressive. More recent work is reported in von Harrison and Reay (1983).

Close attention to organisational detail is also evident in the excellent paper by Trovato and Bucher (1980), who assigned 69 children to three groups: peer tutoring only, peer tutoring with home-based reinforcement, and control. SRA materials were used for the experimental groups, supplemented with additional reading materials over a 15-week programme in seven public schools. Both reading accuracy and reading comprehension were significantly increased by peer tutoring in comparison to the control group, and the addition of home-based reinforcement doubled this increase. The overall measured gain in oral reading based on standardised testing was 0.19 years for the control group and 1.27 years for the peer tutoring with home-based reinforcement group. A more recent review on the efficacy of peer and cross-age tutoring programmes is offered by Gredler (1985), but this is limited in scope, citing only 19 references.

Extension to younger tutors

It has been known for some years that pre-school children can effectively modify the behaviour of siblings and friends in the domestic environment (see Strain 1981 for details). A more recent development has been the deployment of children of such tender years actually to train their peers in desired behaviour.

An example here is the work of Goldstein and Wickstrom (1986) who taught two non-handicapped pre-schoolers strategies to facilitate interaction during free play with three handicapped peers who attended the same nursery (pre-school facility). The two tutors were 4 years of age and of normal intelligence while the three tutees were aged 3 or 4 years, and were diagnosed as behaviour disordered while two were also developmentally delayed. Tutor training was conducted out of the room for 15 minutes per day. Specific strategies were practised during training, being introduced one at a time using a direct instruction approach. There was subsequently some teacher prompting of strategy use during free play. The intervention had immediate effects for all three tutees, and at follow-up there had been no regression in the behaviour of the tutees despite an abrupt decrease in teacher prompting of the tutors. The authors note that using peers as intervention agents may have a positive impact on the generalisation and maintenance of interaction skills.

A similar project is reported by Lobato (1985), except in this case the developmentally normal tutors aged 3 to 7 years of age worked with a handicapped sibling. Training was designed to give the tutors factual explanations, information and support. Positive effects were evident in the tutors' role play responses and attitudes to their handicapped siblings, but there is no evidence of more substantial behavioural change. Nevertheless, the ambition and initiative demonstrated by the mounting of projects of this sort must be applauded, and other projects involving very young children are reported later in this chapter ('Tutors with special needs').

Extension to other curriculum areas

We have already referred to what amounts to tutoring in social skills undertaken by very young children with a difficult tutee group, and this approach was taken further by Lancioni (1982), who used normal children as teachers of social responses including delayed imitation, co-operative play and verbalisation of positive comments to withdrawn mentally retarded peers in an integrated school setting. The tutors were trained using modelling and role play, and subsequently achieved substantial success, which generalised to other settings and other children.

In addition to work in curriculum areas already described, peer tutors have been used to teach motor skills to other children. In the reading field, much early peer tutoring work concentrated on fairly basic reading skill areas, such as word recognition or oral reading. Sindelar (1982) reports an extension of this into the peer tutoring of comprehension skills: 53 primary (elementary) school disabled readers were assigned to one of four groups. A 'hypothesis-test' instructional strategy and materials originally devised for use by teachers were utilised in two groups, one comprising children tutored by peers and the other comprising children tutored in small groups by teachers. Two other groups were peer tutored in oral reading and word recognition. When subsequently assessed on a cloze measure of comprehension, both the 'hypothesis-test' groups scored significantly higher than the word recognition group. The cross-age tutors had administered the hypothesis-test programme as successfully as did the teachers working with small groups.

Reciprocal tutoring

Another project which targets reading comprehension is reciprocal tutoring. As we have already noted, a large age or ability differential between tutor and tutee is not *necessarily* essential for effective tutoring, particularly in basic skill areas. However, the tutoring process is a subtle and complex one, even when targeted on a basic and apparently fairly mechanistic skill. Recently, some workers have introduced the concept of 'reciprocal teaching', with the roles of tutor and tutee alternated in a situation where there is little differential between their abilities, and in some cases have applied this to complex curriculum areas such as reading comprehension.

Pigott *et al.* (1986) report on the effects of reciprocal peer tutoring together with group contingencies on the arithmetic performance of elementary (primary) school children. The arithmetic performance of 12 under-achieving pupils increased during the intervention to a level indistinguishable from their classmates, and these gains were maintained at 12-week follow-up. Furthermore, the students who participated in the project increased their amount of peer affiliation with other treatment group members. Various aspects of peer tutoring operations (i.e. peer instruction, observation, evaluation and reinforcement) were converted into four roles ('coach', 'score-keeper', 'referee', 'manager'). Each member of a team of four accepted one of the roles every day, and the roles rotated day-by-day as the children carried out routine arithmetic drill which no doubt would otherwise have been amazingly boring.

Palincsar and Brown (1986) describe a procedure which they also name 'reciprocal teaching', in which a teacher and a small group of students focus on a designated task but take turns assuming the role of teacher. Four goals or roles are shared by the group: predicting, question generating, summarising and clarifying. These roles are rotated round the group. Initially the teacher models much of the behaviour appropriate to the goals and roles, but before long other children acquire the requisite skills and assume the mantle of 'reciprocal teachers'. Subsequently, the authors went on to train peer tutors to lead new groups. Evaluation results and the range of application described are both impressive. At the time of writing, Palincsar and Brown were experimenting with the use of the procedure with non-readers, in a mixed group of readers and non-readers.

Tutors with special needs

As research accumulates on the benefits accruing to *tutors* as a result of tutoring experiences, a number of workers have developed projects with a *primary aim* of achieving social and academic benefits for potential tutors with learning or behaviour problems. An interesting paper on the deployment of under-achieving pupils as tutors is presented by Bar-Eli and Raviv (1982). This approach was taken even further by Custer and Osguthorpe (1983), who sought to improve the social acceptance of mentally handicapped pupils by arranging for them to tutor their non-handicapped peers in sign language. Following eight weeks of tutoring, interaction between handicapped and non-handicapped pupils was observed to have increased from 5 to 46 per cent of available free play time. Sign language tests showed that the handicapped students retained an average of 94 per cent of the signs they had learnt for tutoring purposes during the project, while non-handicapped students retained an average of 99 per cent of the signs they had learned.

Osguthorpe was also involved as second author in a study with Scruggs (1986) in which both learning-disabled and behaviour-disordered first to sixth graders participated in a cross-age tutoring programme. In a project in which handicapped pupils alternated tutor and tutee roles, the subjects showed significant gains in reading test scores compared to control groups, although there was no evidence of superior attitude change in the tutoring group.

The use of tutoring as a therapeutic device with tutors with emotional and behavioural problems has been as popular, if not more popular, than the use of tutors with learning difficulties. An interesting example of a variant of this approach with very young children is found in a study by Sainato et al. (1986), who examined the effects of assigning a classroom manager's role to three withdrawn kindergarten pupils on their frequency of social interaction and their sociometric standing. Results showed that when these withdrawn children were placed in the managerial (monitorial) role, they initiated more positive social interaction and were the recipients of many more positive and significantly fewer negative social overtures from their peers. Follow-up data from a later time when these children were no longer accorded managerial status suggested partial maintenance of treatment effects.

The deployment of adolescents with behaviour difficulties as cross-age tutors has been undertaken by a number of workers. Stowitschek et al. (1982) used behaviour-disordered adolescents as peer tutors to coach spelling, with immediate and generalised effects. Maher (1982) used conduct problem adolescents as cross-age tutors for elementary (primary) school mentally retarded pupils. When compared to students in control groups who had received alternative 'treatments', the cross-age tutors improved significantly on their grades in social science and language arts, and had significantly reduced rates of truancy and disciplinary referrals. These changes were maintained during the follow-up period.

Further work of this kind was reported by Maher in 1984. Pupils classified as emotionally disturbed in the special education programme of a high school in an urban school district served as cross-age tutors to pupils enrolled in the special education programme of an elementary school in the same school district, all of whom were classified as educable mentally retarded (EMR), and tutoring was provided twice a week over a ten-week period, covering the curriculum areas of reading, language and mathematics. The description of this ambitious programme is clear and detailed and is recommended for practising teachers wishing to replicate this work. Results were impressive.

Tutors raised their mean completion percentage of their own academic assignments from 62 per cent at base line to 95 per cent during intervention, stabilising at 93 per cent during follow-up. The tutors' percentage of items correct on tests and quizzes likewise increased from 56 to 88 per cent, stabilising at 85 per cent during follow-up. Disciplinary referrals of tutors fell from an average of six during the base line period to two during the intervention period, stabilising at one during follow-up. The tutees benefited too! Their percentage of completion of academic assignments was raised from 66 per cent to 94 per cent, stabilising at 90 per cent during follow-up, while their percentage of items correct on tests and quizzes was raised from 65 to 88 per cent, stabilising at 82 per cent during follow-up.

In 1985, Scruggs *et al.* were able to produce a review of reports on peer tutoring with behaviourally and emotionally disordered students which covered 17 studies. Reading was the most frequently chosen area of intervention. Overall results suggested that tutoring undoubtedly exerted a positive effect on the academic functioning of the tutee, and under certain circumstances could influence the academic functioning of the tutor. Social relations in the tutoring dyad and attitudes towards the content area being tutored also frequently improved, although generally improved social functioning and elevated self-concepts were found in relatively few of the research studies. However, given the reported effectiveness of the work of Maher (1984), we may expect better designed studies increasingly to yield positive results in these latter aspects also.

DEVELOPMENTS IN THE UNITED KINGDOM

The two major figures in peer tutoring in the United Kingdom in the 1970s have continued to be productive. In Newcastle, Carol Fitz-Gibbon and her students and associates have continued to use and research peer tutoring in a great variety of contexts. One of the more recent papers (Fitz-Gibbon and Reay 1982) describes the use of peer tutoring in foreign language teaching in an urban comprehensive school.

Meanwhile, Sinclair Goodlad's work in involving undergraduates from the Imperial College of Science and Technology at London University to help tutor science, mathematics and engineering in local schools has continued unabated. In an article (1985) Goodlad reported subjective evaluation results from four years of this kind of work.

Replies to questionnaires from almost 3,000 pupils, almost 300 tutors and 130 teachers indicated that 64 per cent of the pupils found lessons easier to follow, 95 per cent of the tutors felt they had gained useful practice in communicating scientific ideas, and 66 per cent of the teachers felt that lessons were more enjoyable when the tutors were present.

In addition, as we have already noted, completely new movements in peer tutoring have been taking shape in the United Kingdom.

Pause, Prompt and Praise

The 1980s saw a great surge of interest in parental involvement in children's reading, with particular interest being aroused by semi-structured techniques which lay somewhere between the traditional *laissez-faire* practice of the English primary school and the highly structured programmed methods of the teaching of reading by para-professionals which had emerged in the United States. An example of this was the 'Pause, Prompt and Praise' technique which was originally developed in New Zealand. (Further details of this technique are available in Topping and Wolfendale 1985.)

These semi-structured techniques had obvious appeal in terms of ease of transmission to non-professional tutors, and it was not long before Pause, Prompt and Praise was deployed on a cross-age tutor basis by workers at the University of Birmingham. Wheldall and Mettem (1985) reported on the use of eight 16-year-old low-achieving pupils as cross-age tutors for retarded readers aged 12 years, over eight weeks for 24 tutorial sessions with two matched control groups, one tutored by untrained tutors and one who read silently without tutoring. The experimental group made a mean gain of 6 months in reading accuracy by the end of the programme, while the group that received untrained tutoring made a mean gain of 2.4 months and the group which had read silently without tutoring made a mean gain of 1.8 months. (This work has subsequently been developed by Wheldall and his associates and students at the Centre for Child Study, and further details of recent work are available from there. See Chapter 8.)

Paired reading

This much more widespread semi-structured technique for non-professional involvement in reading tutoring was first used for peer tutoring projects in the early 1980s. The technique has the advantage of allowing free access to reading materials so long as they are within the *tutor's* reading competence, which tends to facilitate greater flexibility and enjoyment in the tutoring pair. Early reports were those of Winter and Low (1984) and Carrick-Smith (most easily accessible in Topping and Wolfendale 1985). Since then there have been two further papers by Alan Low and his co-workers, and a succession of reports which have appeared in the *Paired Reading Bulletin* published by the Kirklees Paired Reading Project in West Yorkshire (see Chapter 8).

A report on peer tutored Paired Reading has also emanated from New Zealand (Limbrick *et al.* 1985). Results have been extremely positive, with both tutors and tutees improving on criterion- and norm-referenced reading tests. Studies which have incorporated baseline, control and follow-up components also yield encouraging results. The attitudes of tutors and tutees to their joint experiences are largely positive. There is some evidence that peer tutoring in Paired Reading can be as effective as parent tutoring, particularly with respect to the improvements made by the *tutors* (see Townsend and Topping 1986).

Articles summarising some of the considerable progress in this area are begining to appear. Thus, Winter (1986) reviews five such projects and offers guidelines for organising projects. Topping (1987b) summarises outcome data from ten projects run consecutively (i.e. unselective) in one Local Education Authority (School District). Results were various, but all results were positive, and the best results were staggering. The field of peer tutored Paired Reading still awaits the first critical academic review of research, but there is no doubt that it holds great promise. It is unlikely that this particular mode of peer tutoring will prove in time to show better results than some of the more carefully organised and well structured United States projects of different format, but the Paired Reading approach has the advantage of ease of organisation and training of tutors, and thus does prove to have considerable cost-effectiveness.

A further interesting development is the use of peer tutoring with adults, whereby non-professional adults who can read use the Paired Reading technique to tutor adults with literacy problems with whom they are in naturalistic everyday contact. Thus, adults with literacy problems have been tutored by spouses, relatives, workmates, friends and in some cases by their own children. This use of the Paired Reading technique has also proved effective, and further details of outcomes are available in Scoble *et al.* (1987). (A training pack to help workers wishing to explore this field has been produced. See Chapter 8.)

CONCLUSION

The extravagant claims for tutoring made by Bloom (1984) with respect to the attainment of the 'two-sigma effect' appear to be largely substantiated by the research we have reviewed. Gains for tutors as well as tutees are widely reported, involving increased attainment in the subject area of tutoring and in positive attitudes to each other and to the subject area. Generalised improvements in behaviour and in self-concept have proved more difficult to demonstrate, but in the latter case this may be due to problems of adequate measurement, and in the former case the better designed studies are beginning to show good results. No doubter can now rationally oppose peer tutoring on the grounds that it is not effective.

Nevertheless, because peer tutoring is effective in general, that does not mean it is bound to be effective right there where you are. A number of studies have not produced significant results, and these tend to be rarely discussed or reported. When establishing a peer tutoring project, particularly for the first time, it is essential that it is most carefully organised and that evaluation research is built in. Methods for evaluating peer tutoring projects are discussed in the next chapter.

7

Evaluating a Project

Considerable emphasis has been placed on evaluating peer tutoring projects. Just because spectacular results have been achieved in some places, it doesn't guarantee that *you* will too. Especially with your first effort, you need to know how successful you have been and how you can improve effectiveness even more in the future. Then after a few projects, just when you think you've got it all off pat, circumstances will change and dictate a different kind of project, so evaluation remains just as essential. In any event, evaluation will help convince sceptics of the value of what you are doing. And evaluating yourself is a lot more comfortable than some outsider doing it. Most importantly, you will find the tutors and tutees very eager to be told how they've done — so you'd better have something concrete to tell them!

One of the great virtues of peer tutoring is its cost-effectiveness, i.e. what the tutors and tutees get out of it for the time and effort put in by the professionals who are managing and co-ordinating the project. Thus it would be nonsensical for the professionals to spend a vast amount of their time evaluating a project. However, a small amount of time is worth devoting to this task. This chapter details some of the ways of going about it. You will need to choose the ways you think are best and easiest for your own situation.

THE PURPOSE OF EVALUATION

Before you can determine whether or not your project was a success, you need to be clear about why you did it in the first place. Project co-ordinators often have a wide range of objectives in mind when they embark on a particular initiative, but they do not always articulate these consciously. To some extent of course, the setting of objectives for a first project in a novel setting will always involve a lot of guesswork. It is not until one becomes relatively experienced in running peer tutoring projects that one can set objectives with a degree of precision and exactitude in full expectation that most of them have a reasonable chance of being met. A point which must be borne in mind is that the programme objectives espoused by the co-ordinator may be quite different from those of the tutors, tutees, or other relevant professional colleagues. Thus, while you may be out to raise reading attainments, the tutees may be out to have a good time, the tutors may be wanting to feel grandiose and powerful, while the school principal may be wanting the project to reduce conflict in the playground between two sets of pupils, and traditionalist colleagues may be wanting the project to fall apart at the seams to justify their conviction that such new-fangled ideas are doomed to failure and the old ways are undoubtedly the best. Different people have different objectives, some spoken and some unspoken, and you are most unlikely to be able to meet all of them.

Nevertheless, some attempt is necessary from *your* perspective, to be clear about the criteria you would set by which the project would be judged a success or a failure — in terms of the impact on your desire to repeat the exercise on another occasion. You need to specify your objectives in clear, precise and *observable* terms. Sweeping aims described in lofty philosophical prose are useless for this purpose. Warm, 'fuzzy', emotional aspirations will not do. You need, during the event, to be able to *see* whether the objectives are being met — they have to be defined in operational terms.

It is all very well saying that evaluation must proceed from the setting of objectives for the project, but what are the objectives for doing the evaluation? We have already mentioned the need to be able to demonstrate effectiveness in order to be able to improve effectiveness. Evaluation evidence may convince your colleagues of the value of peer tutoring, and encourage them to emulate your good work. Beyond that, it may be that your good works will disseminate to other schools, whereby you will indirectly have a profound effect on the education of a very large number of students. The immediate practical pressure for the availability of tangible evaluation evidence is undoubtedly the demand from the grass roots. The tutors and tutees will value their own feelings about how well they have done. However, you are the expert, so they will value your opinion on how well they have done even more — and if all you have to give them is vague well-meaning platitudes, your credibility (and the programme) is going to suffer.

Finally of course, a major purpose of evaluation is reinforcement for yourself. A vague feeling that the project 'went OK' is unlikely to give you the confidence and reassurance you need to launch forth into the brave new world of peer tutoring. If you have more concrete data about the success of the project, which is independent of your own views, you will feel you are working from a more solid foundation. There is also the interesting effect of 'deferred reinforcement' — if you can present scientific data on your effectiveness as a planner and co-ordinator of peer tutor projects, this is unlikely to do your promotion prospects any harm!

Peer tutoring projects are like life itself — none of them are ever entirely predictable. It is thus almost inevitable some of your objectives will not be met, but that you will find teasingly vague evidence of serendipitous gains in areas where you least expected it. Don't worry, it's the same for everyone.

TYPES OF EVALUATION

There are two main types of evaluation, 'Process' (or Formative) evaluation and 'Product' (or Summative or Outcome) evaluation. Summative or Outcome evaluation looks solely at the end-product of a project, without looking closely at how effective each of the various aspects of the organisation and methods of the project were in achieving this goal. These latter questions are the focus of Formative evaluation, so named because the data gathered enable you to re-form a better project next time, or even adjust the current one as you go along.

A number of reports of projects in the literature include no data about outcomes, but merely constitute a description of how the project worked. This is all very well up to a point, and is an essential aspect of an overall evaluation, but the description itself needs to be precise and have some quantitative aspects. How many meetings were held, and what was the attendance rate by different categories of personnel? What was the participation rate of tutors and tutees, divided into pre-launch and post-launch drop-out rates, as well as frequency in regularity of contracted contacts made during the project? Was the desired behaviour demonstrated by tutors, tutees and project co-ordinators? Did the tutors actually implement the tutoring procedures in which they had been trained, or could the improvement shown by the tutees be attributed solely to the effect of extra individual attention? Did the project co-ordinator monitor tutoring sessions regularly and frequently as expected? Were tutoring materials prepared in good time and always brought to sessions? Was record keeping completed as required, and were all records subsequently collated for analysis?

The fundamental question with the Process aspect of project evaluation is whether or not the project actually operated as planned and intended. Without process data, outcome data cannot be construed to reflect upon the effectiveness of the programme procedures. On the other hand, even a quantitative description of project process remains no more than that — it tells us whether the project was put into operation as intended, but does not tell us whether it 'worked'.

RESEARCH DESIGN

Evaluation research is basically about detecting change (and preferably measuring the degree of change). The obvious thing is to apply your measure(s) at the start of the project and again at the end of the project to the children who take part (Pre-Post Test Design). But if your measure is not norm-referenced (standardised), you will have no way of telling whether the children would have made the pre-post changes anyway, irrespective of the project. Even if your measure is norm-referenced (like a standardised reading test), unless your results are spectacularly better than 'normal' rates of gain, you still won't have proof that the children could only have made those gains with the help of the project. Standardisations refer to averages for hundreds of children from all over the country.

However, the standardisation may not be immediately relevant to a small group of children with peculiar attainment profiles in your particular educational establishment. So you really need to compare the progress of your project students with the progress of a similar local group who have not been involved in the project. If you offer involvement in the project to 20 tutees, and only ten finally participate, you can use the ten 'drop-outs' as a 'comparison' group. But the ten drop-outs are not a true 'control' group because they have self-selected not to participate, and factors which incline them to do that are likely to be associated with the factors causing their difficulties. Nevertheless, it is better to have a comparison group than not, so you should apply your measure(s) pre- and post-project to both groups. Don't try to make out your comparison group is a control group, though. To get a true control group, you would list your 20 children, then allocate them randomly to 'control' or 'project' groups (by tossing a coin or using random number tables). Both groups would be pretested, then only the 'project' group invited to participate. However, not all of them would agree, so you would then have:—

Control Group   Experimental Group

   n = 10   Participating   n = 5
                       Not participating n = 5

After post-testing all 20 children at the end of the project, what comparisons can you make? Strictly speaking, you should compare all the 'controls' with all the 'experimentals', whether the latter participated or not. This builds in conservatism to any claims you might make on the data, but does allow you to use quite stringent parametric tests of statistical significance without invalidating their underlying assumptions. Alternatively, or in addition, you can make a three-way analysis comparing the three groups, but you will only be able to apply non-parametric tests of statistical significance. In any event, the numbers quoted here in the experimental sub-groups are so small as to make comparisons of doubtful validity. An absolute minimum sample size of ten is desirable to have any real confidence in your results.

So far we have talked about fairly classical research design. But there are alternative approaches, which can be nearly as 'scientifically' acceptable and which can prove easier to do, especially where existing data can be utilised. If for the students concerned there has been in the past a regular routine of applying attainment tests, historical data may be available for the project group. This enables you to scrutinise the fluctuations in progress in the past, and see how the gains during the project compare. This is called the (Interrupted) Time Series Design (Figure 7.1). Acceleration during the project is fairly clearly evident in relation to previous rates of progress. Parametric tests are not applicable, however.

Even better, and demanding little extra work, would be the inclusion of similar data from a comparison group (Figure 7.2). Here, acceleration in the project group is again evident, and also illustrated is how that relates to the progress of the other children in the year group, clarifying how the gap is narrowed. Again, remember this is a comparison group, not a control group. A randomly selected true control group would have to be determined right at the start of the Time Series, and few schools go in for this degree of forward planning! Also, loss of subjects from the groups over the years (sample attrition) may do funny things to the results. Your comparison group

Figure 7.1: (Interrupted) Time Series Design

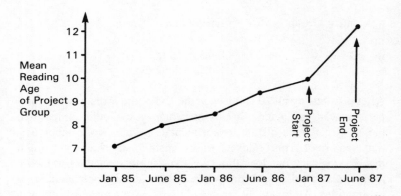

Figure 7.2: Time Series with Comparison Series

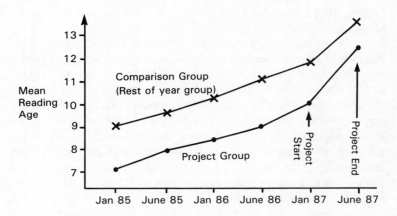

could be the rest of the year group, children who are invited to participate in the project but refuse, children with less severe educational problems, or any other groups with whom comparison would be interesting and valid. A further advantage of the Time Series design is that data can readily continue to be accumulated after the end of the project, the Time Series extended, and very interesting long-term follow-up data generated.

As will already be evident, one of the problems with true control groups is that their use involves denying a service or facility to people who clearly seem to be in need of it. It can be argued that until you have demonstrated that the project has worked satisfactorily by using the control group, you don't actually know whether you are denying the control group anything worthwhile, but this contention does not tend to go down well with teachers.

A design which is useful in getting round this problem is the Regression Discontinuity Design. Where a limited amount of a service or facility is available, there is often felt to be a moral obligation that *all* those in greatest need receive the service. If enough service is available to meet the needs of those who are worst off, but still leave some spare capacity, the limited surplus service may be extended to the larger band of those whose needs are less severe. But how to allocate the limited surplus to this large group? Arguably, random selection for project inclusion is the fairest way to go about it for this mid-band of students. If the project workers are unhappy with this, a fixed arbitrary criterion on some measure can be set to determine inclusion or non-inclusion for this mid-band, e.g. specific and exact reading age. So your final results can be charted as in Figure 7.3. Or the results can be charted in regression terms (see Figure 7.4 overleaf).

Figure 7.3: Regression Discontinuity Design

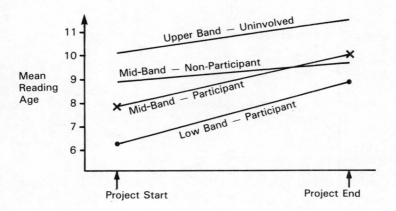

Finally, one further design is probably worth mentioning, which also gets round the ethical problems involving using control groups. This is the Multiple Baseline Design (Figure 7.5). If a larger group

Figure 7.4: Regression Lines at Sample Boundary

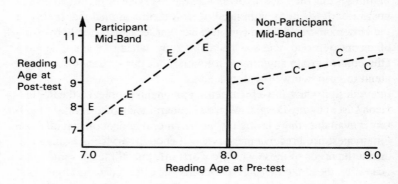

E = Experimental   C = Control

of potential clients exists than can be serviced at one time, they may have to be serviced by two consecutive projects. Where one half of the clients have to be serviced first, and the second later, it is reasonable and fair to allocate to 'early' and 'late' groups randomly. The gains of the 'early' group can be compared in the short run to the progress of the 'late' group. Subsequently, variations in procedure can be applied to one or other group, and gains compared within and between groups.

Figure 7.5: Multiple Baseline Design

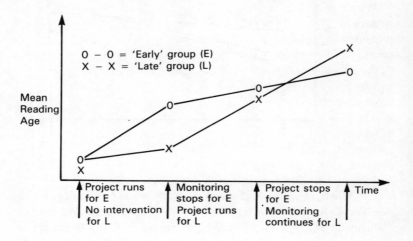

If you want to get really complicated, you could combine features of these designs. Other, usually more complex, designs are also possible. Whatever you choose to do, some attempt to guard against the Hawthorne Effect is necessary — the effect whereby the clients of an intervention show brief improvement purely because some attention is being paid to them and there is some element of novelty about the proceedings, quite irrespective of the actual nature of the intervention. Another possible source of embarrassment is the 'John Henry Effect' — where the control group, alerted to the fact that somebody considers them to be in need but is not providing anything for them, determines to improve anyway, and does so without apparent outside intervention.

SUBJECTS OF EVALUATION

Initially, the most frequently cited major objective of peer tutoring pro-grammes was to raise the attainment in a particular curriculum area of the tutees. As it became clear that the peer tutoring process had a beneficial effect on the expertise in that curriculum area of the *tutors* also, as much attention came to be paid to measuring the gains of the tutors as to those of the tutees. Furthermore, as project co-ordinators became aware of even wider possibilities, measures were increasingly applied to the attitudes, behaviour and self-concept of both parties, both with reference to the tutored curriculum area and to other curriculum areas. It seems likely that the variety and range of evaluative questions it is possible to pose about peer tutoring is infinitely expandable.

What is *not* infinitely expandable is the project co-ordinator's time, so decisions have to be made about how many and which evaluative measures are going to be applied to tutor and tutee respectively. Of course there are many other personnel who are in a sense participant — the project co-ordinator, other teaching staff, non-teaching staff, parents and other members of the extended family, and so on. All of these are potentially data providers, if the impact of the programme is to be looked at in its very widest sense. But again, the practicalities of the situation are likely severely to restrict the range of evaluation subjects who can pragmatically be used as data providers. Nevertheless, much of what is said below relates equally to tutors, tutees and other personnel who are in some way related to or participant in the project.

MEASURES

There are various basic requirements of any measures you seek to use. Economy of cost in materials and of time in administration and scoring are two obvious considerations. The measure needs to be reliable, in the sense of not being susceptible to wild, random fluctuations or erratic guesswork. It also needs to be valid, i.e. one must be assured that it actually measures what it is purporting to measure. Of equal importance, it needs to be relevant to the processes in question. Thus a phonic skills teaching programme would probably not be relevantly evaluated by application of a reading test containing a very high proportion of irregular 'sight' words. Last, but by no means least, the measure must generate information which is analysable. A vast quantity of impressionistic opinion may be fascinating to the project organisers, but will not enable them to communicate their findings to others in a clear and credible way.

Individual versus group tests

The peer tutoring experience is nothing if not personal, involving as it does the development of a one-to-one relationship which persists over time and hopefully develops in quality, being characterised by rich and detailed feedback from tutor to tutee. During peer tutoring, problems tend to be solved jointly as much as individually, and help is more or less always at hand. The relationship and the speed of progress through curriculum materials, which may themselves be completely individualised, is highly idiosyncratic.

To attempt to assess the impact of an experience of this kind by the use of some sort of group test, wherein the tutees sit in isolation in serried ranks and wrestle without help with some standardised task, seems logically to be something of a nonsense — or is it?

If you wish to determine whether peer tutoring has improved the ability of tutor or tutee to function in *that kind of situation*, an individually administered measure would seem essential. But if you are anticipating that the peer tutoring experience will produce results which will spread and endure *outside of* the tutoring situation, then the application of a group measure could be construed as a usefully stringent measure of generalisation. However, it is perhaps worth remembering that whatever the reliability of the group test quoted in the manual may be, with a small and idiosyncratically selected group of children with learning difficulties, reliability may be actually considerably less. Where group and individual tests have been used, correlation between the two kinds of test result has often been poor. While the use of group tests may show substantial rates of gain taking the project group as a whole, individual results may seem so meaningless as to render the worth of the exercise somewhat doubtful.

Norm-referenced versus criterion-referenced

Norm-referenced tests allow a student's performance to be compared with that of many others in various parts of the country. Criterion-referenced tests allow a student's performance to be compared with his own previous performance. The first compares the student with other students, and the second compares the student's performance with a pre-determined criterion of skill acquisition. All tests have inherent problems. They may provoke anxiety in some students, making individual results largely meaningless. For others, the unreality and apparent purposelessness of the exercise produces equally strange results.

Norm-referenced tests tend to have more pretentions than criterion-referenced tests, and are thus more easily criticised. In many tests, the content is dated and of doubtful interest to specific sub-groups. The standardisation data may be neither recent nor localised, and the data on supposed reliability and validity may be based on very small numbers. The structure of the test may itself be problematic, and you may find in some cases that answering only one or two more questions correctly produces a substantial shift in standardised score — the briefer the test, the more likely it is to suffer from this problem. In some cases, there may be grave doubts about the cross-reliability of the supposedly 'parallel' forms of the test. Some evaluators have tried to get round this by allocating forms at random at pre-test and the remaining forms at random at post-test. Another problem is that standardised tests may be used on a pre-post basis to evaluate a relatively short project, when they were not designed for repeated use in short time spans in this kind of application.

In the reading area, standardised tests have included tasks of: word/picture matching, individual word recognition, phonically regular word recognition, oral sentence reading, oral prose reading coupled with comprehension and recall questions, silent reading of signs, menus and directions coupled with comprehension questions, silent reading of continuous prose with cloze tasks, silent reading of sentences with multiple choice cloze tasks, and (would you believe!) having children read a real book and then answer questions on it.

103

By contrast, the advantage of criterion-referenced tests is that they can much more flexibly reflect the reality of the tutoring curriculum. Their disadvantage is that comparison with national norms is no longer possible, and the absence of that vast, distant quasi-'control' group means that much more emphasis must be placed on achieving an adequate evaluation design. Basically, a criterion-referenced test checks whether the tutees have learnt what they have been taught. While this may be simple and logical, they may not give information on how well the tutees can generalise new skills to other areas, unless this is built into the structure of the test. Nor may it be easy to obtain any idea of whether the student is accelerating at a rate that will eventually enable them to catch up with the norm.

In the reading area, Informal Reading Inventories are a good example of this sort of device. An alternative possibility is some kind of cloze test based on curriculum material standard to the educational establishment, for instance the core reading scheme. A word recognition test could be constructed from lists of high frequency words, or from designated social sight vocabulary.

Where a school is using a criterion-referenced measure of its own devising, it is worthwhile 'piloting' it with a relevant sub-group in the locality first. A check on the stability of the measure with a normal sample in the school on a test-re-test, no-intervention basis would do, but would not necessarily reflect the stability of the measure with a sub-sample of 'abnormal' students. The best bet may be a test-re-test, no-intervention pilot run with the project group to give Time Series and/or reliability data specific to the situation prior to the project. In any event, where standardised or criterion-referenced tests are in use, pre- and post-project measures should be carried out by the same person, to ensure that any bias (particularly to generosity in scoring) or other 'tester effects' will be the same on both occasions.

Instead of a straight attainment measure, some workers choose to evaluate by the deployment of a battery of 'diagnostic' tests. Some of these, such as 'miscue analysis' in the field of reading, can give useful information with practical implications for teaching and reflect qualitative changes in the learning style of students. However, other diagnostic tests are based on elaborate theoretical frameworks for which there is little sound empirical evidence, and may result in the drawing of no conclusions at all or the drawing of conclusions which have no practical import. Where sub-skills are to be measured as part of an evaluation with 'diagnostic' overtones, it is important that the real existence of those sub-skills and their practical relevance to the overall educational process is unquestioned.

Educational versus social gains

Most peer tutor projects are organised around the primary objective of achieving gains in attainment in tutees and tutors, with social and emotional gains tending to be regarded as fortuitous by-products. However, as we have already seen, some professionals are increasingly using peer tutoring primarily for the achievement of social and emotional objectives, usually in the tutor, although the evidence for the effectiveness of this approach is as yet somewhat equivocal.

If social or emotional gains figure largely among your objectives for the project, you are likely to attempt some sort of measure of this, although to do so in such an area is fraught with difficulty, and doubts about reliability and validity will be great. Again, consideration is needed of whether these measures are to apply to tutee, tutor or both.

A crude naturalistic indicator of improved behaviour might be a reduced incidence of disciplinary referrals. There may be evidence of reductions in bullying, fighting and vandalism. Where data on these are not already collected through existing record systems, it may be worthwhile to have adults in regular contact with target children complete some form of rating, or a more specific checklist of problem behaviours, or one of the more generalised observational assessments of problem behaviour such as a Bristol Social Adjustment Guide (Stott 1974). Direct observation with reference to some structured schedule is always valuable, but has the disadvantage of being very time-consuming, so it is usually necessary to ask adults to make observations only in times when they would in any event be in contact with the relevant children. Of course, reductions in some of the more dramatic problem behaviours should not be routinely expected. In most cases, it will be interesting merely to see whether tutoring partners interact with each other more outside of the tutoring situation for the duration of the project, and at follow-up beyond. Naturalistic indicators such as choice of peers for teams and activity groups can be most revealing.

Beyond direct observation, there are a range of other measures, which may have the virtue of seeming quicker and easier, but which also raise more serious questions about relationship to everyday reality. Some form of sociometry is a particular favourite, on a before and after basis, to discern whether post-project tutoring pairs show any greater preference for each other on paper and pencil completion of preference lists. Attempts can be made to tap the more generalised attitudes of tutoring pairs to each other and the world in general, and this could be done verbally on an individual or group basis, or with no fewer threats to reliability via some form of simple questionnaire of controlled readability. Some project co-ordinators like to use paper and pencil 'tests' of self-concept or self-image, but some fairly erratic results have emerged from such exercises from time to time.

With all these measures, the issue of generalisation needs to be addressed. Is it enough to have some form of evidence that social and emotional gains have occurred which are specific to the tutoring pair or the tutoring situation, or is it reasonable to expect these gains to generalise to ordinary classroom sessions, free-play periods, or perhaps even to the community and home environments beyond the school boundary?

Behavioural versus attitudinal data

Our discussion of the difficulties of evaluating social and emotional gains highlights a continuing quandary in research of this kind — the inconsistent relationship between what people feel and what they do. Considerable attention has been paid in education to so called 'affective outcomes', the reasoning being that unless children learn to like what they learn to do, they are unlikely to go on doing it once they leave the school precincts. Differences sometimes arise between workers in the field, where one group espouses direct quantitative recording of behaviour and another is wholly preoccupied with what the participants in a given project say they feel about it.

In fact, of course, neither kind of datum is wholly valid by itself, and it is useful to gather a mixture of kinds of datum wherever possible to obtain a fuller picture of what actually happened in a project from a variety of perspectives.

Behavioural measures can relate to either the process or outcome aspects of evaluation. They may include observation of required or desired behaviours during the project, in comparison with such behaviours occurring naturally during a baseline period or in comparison with those behaviours occurring spontaneously in a control group. Behaviour cannot be observed continuously, and some form of subject-sampling, time-sampling or fixed-interval-sampling may be employed. In these cases, it is important to check on inter-observer reliability. It is of course possible to attempt to assess behavioural change in a much looser way by asking (almost casual) observers to complete rating scales, but these are much less reliable and suffer from a 'halo' effect. As we have already seen, there may be naturalistic indicators which are superficially behavioural but which certainly have affective and attitudinal overtones — like truancy and lateness rates.

Methodology of assessing 'attitudes' is problematic. The whole notion of 'attitudes' is highly nebulous. If you want people's *feelings* about the project, ask for them directly, but don't expect them necessarily to bear much relationship to the participants' actual behaviour or even the gains shown in attainment. On the other hand, if you want people's observations of what participants actually *did*, ask for that directly, giving a 'no observations made' option. But do avoid confusing the two by asking for woolly generalised 'attitudes' or 'opinions'.

The views of the major participants in the project (tutors, tutees, co-ordinators, and other professionals) should always be elicited. To rely simply on primitive instruments such as tests is to risk missing the texture of the reality of what happened. The participants will probably offer more process insights than summative conclusions, but the former must not be neglected. Soliciting participant opinions serves not only to gather information, but also to clarify the information-giver's mind on the subject, resolve any residual practical problems, and very often to recharge and commit the participants to continued effort.

A group meeting for all participants at the end of the project (or at the end of the initial 'push') is often a good idea. This could be (audio-) tape-recorded for more detailed analysis later (although an analysis of such loose data could prove a massive task). If time is available, individual interviews with at least the tutors along some semi-structured format is desirable. Similar interviews with the tutees and professionals are desirable, but should preferably be carried out by an 'outsider' to the project if they are to be remotely objective.

Realistically, time constraints and/or the need to have readily analysable data often drive people into using some form of questionnaire. However, there are very large doubts about the reliability and validity of responses to paper-and-pencil measures. In the construction of questionnaires, the project leaders must decide which questions are important to them, but the device must be structured to eliminate any possibility of leading respondents into giving a particular answer. A multiple-choice format gives easily analysable data, but is crude and simplistic, while an open-ended format is dependent on the free-writing skills of the respondents and yields data which is often difficult to analyse. Some overall index of consumer satisfaction is desirable, and a useful acid test is always the question: 'Would you recommend the project to a friend?'

Lying somewhere in the middle ground between behavioural and attitudinal measures are various techniques of 'self-recording'. Participants may keep simple written records on themselves and/or each other in the form of points, grades, ratings, or general comments or quantitative notes of task completed, time taken, etc. In some projects, participants make audio or video recordings of themselves for later viewing and/or rating by themselves and/or others. This kind of self-evaluation is often valuable for keeping participants on-task.

GENERALISATION AND MAINTENANCE

Are the gains made in the tutoring situation specific to that situation, or do we expect them to generalise — to other situations, to other (untargeted) skills or problems, to other resource materials, or to other tutees or tutors? If we do expect this, how are we to measure it? Most difficult of all, how are we to measure it easily?

The other thorny questoin is that of long-term duration of gains made. Many teaching programmes (particularly in the remedial field) have shown reasonable results in the short-term, but the gains produced have often 'washed out' in comparison to control groups at two year follow-up. So some form of follow-up evaluation is essential, together with follow-up of a control or comparison group. Such an exercise is often made difficult by the loss of subjects from one or both groups — 'sample attrition'. On the other hand, it is also reasonable to ask how long you can sensibly expect a relatively brief and 'lightweight' intervention to continue to demonstrate an impact on the highly complex and cumulative learning process.

Fortunately, where Time Series evaluative data on attainment is routinely collected on a yearly basis in school, follow-up evaluation research is greatly facilitated.

ANALYSIS OF DATA

So far as statistical analysis is concerned, it has already been noted that the use of random allocation to samples usually permits the use of parametric methods (eg 't' tests), while non-random allocation usually implies the use of non-parametric methods (e.g. Wilcoxon tests, Fisher tests, Mann-Whitney tests, Chi-Squared tests, etc.) With random samples, an initial 'feel' for the data gained via a simple scattergram could be followed by an analysis of covariance (ANCOVA) to allow for any initial differences found between experimental and control groups, followed by an analysis of variance (ANOVA), perhaps repeatedly. Correlation analysis is possible, and co-efficients can subsequently be tested for statistical significance, but by and large this is a less 'powerful' procedure, raising inherent doubts about the direction of causative linkages.

There is a great difference between statistical and educational significance, however. Where a very large sample is used, statistical significance is much easier to achieve. Where a very large number of different outcome measures are used, the chances are that one or two will show statistically significant changes irrespective of any real impact of the project. If a project with large samples produces gains which are only just statistically significant, searching questions need to be asked about the *educational* significance of the results. Was it worth all that time and effort for such a small skill increment?

For those unsure of their competence in statistical analysis, or doubting the validity of the procedures, simple comparison of raw data on scattergrams or graphing of shifts in averages for groups gives a ready visual indication of changes. Certainly the data is worth summarising in this sort of way for feedback to the participants, who may be assumed to be statistically unsophisticated.

Evaluation results feedback

One of the disadvantages of complex data analysis is that it takes time, and very often early feedback of evaluation results to the project participants is highly desirable, to renew their commitment and recharge their energies. A simple graph and/or brief table of average scores for the group is probably the best vehicle for this — remember, the results must be understood by the tutees as well. The unreliability of standardised tests makes giving individual test scores to the participants a risky business, and care must be taken throughout not to give undue emphasis to standardised test data as distinct from other types. Any individual scores are probably best given in an individual interview rather than a group meeting situation, if at all. In any event, it is probably best for one person to take responsibility for collating and presenting the evaluation data, or it might lie about on scraps of paper forever.

Evaluation results have a number of other uses as well. Publicity via the local press, professional journals, curriculum bulletins or in-service meetings not only helps to disseminate good practice and help more children, it also serves to boost the morale of the project initiators and participants. The results may be useful to convince sceptics on the school staff, generate a wider interest and produce a more coherent future policy on peer tutoring in the school. The school governors will be interested, as should be various officers of the Education Authority or State Board. A demonstration of cost-effectiveness may elicit more tangible support from administration or elected representatives. Associated services such as library services, advisory services, resource materials centres, and so on, may be drawn into the network of community support by a convincing evaluation report.

And so to the final word. If you get results you don't like, you'll spend hours puzzling over them trying to explain them away. Make sure that if you get results you do like, you spend as much time and energy searching for other factors outside the project that could have produced them. If you don't spot them, someone else might — and probably will!

8

Resource Materials

PRACTICAL MANUALS AND KITS

Given the speed of change in education, by the time you read this book some of the materials below will no longer be available, while new manuals and kits not listed here will have been published. It would be appreciated if readers could notify the author via the publishers of any new items which could be incorporated in this section of the book in subsequent editions.

ERIC numbers here and in the References facilitate retrieval from the Educational Resources Information Center in Washington, DC., with which libraries throughout the world are linked. Some items are not otherwise available.

Deterline, W.A. (1970) *Training and Management of Student Tutors: final report*. (ERIC ED 048133)

Ellson, D.G. 'Programmed Tutoring'. Ellson's highly structured system was initially designed for use by adult para-professional tutors. It covers children aged 6 to 9 years. Further information may be obtained from the Department of Psychology, Indiana University, Bloomington, Indiana 47401

Gartner, A., Kohler, M. and Riessman, F. (1971) *Children Teach Children: learning by teaching*. Harper and Row, New York and London. (This book has a substantial practical section.)

Harrison, G. von 'Structured Tutoring' and 'Companion Study'. Grant von Harrison's individualised programme was originally intended for reading and arithmetic tutoring on a cross-age basis, but has been extended to true age-peer tutoring. Self-instructional materials about the method are available. Manuals for the use of the method in experiential writing and paired associate tasks have also been prepared. Further information is available from the Brigham Young University, Provo, Utah 84601. Distributed in the UK by David Reay, Education, Training & Technology Consultants, 1 Beechwood Avenue, Ryton, Tyne and Wear NE40 3LX. 'Classroom kit' and 'specialist kit' available.

'Homework Helper Programme (New York)'. Program Conspectus. A number of reports including a tutor's manual were available from the co-ordinator of the programme at the Board of Education, Brooklyn, New York 11201. (Other details are retrievable from ERIC under the number ED 035712.)

Klausmeier, H.J., Jeter, J.R. and Nelson, N.J. (1972) *Tutoring Can Be Fun*. Research and Development Centre for Cognitive Learning, Madison, Wisconsin. (This handbook includes procedures, methods and practical exercises.)

Lippitt, P., Eiseman, J.W. and Lippitt, R. 'The Cross-Age Helping Package'. A range of practical materials available from the Institute for Social Research, University of Michigan, PO Box 1248, Ann Arbor, Michigan 48108. Another useful source is: Lippitt, P. (1975) 'Cross-Age Helping Programmes and Suggested Designs Which Have Worked Well in Cross-Age Helping Programmes'. (ERIC ED 108086)

Lundblad, H. and Smith, C.B. (1972) *Tutor Trainer's Handbook*. National Reading Centre Foundation, Washington, D.C. (ERIC ED 068459). A guide for training tutors in adult reading.

Maher, C.A. 'Handicapped Adolescents as Cross-Age Tutors'. The programme manual is available from the author at the Department of School Psychology, Rutgers University, Piscataway, New Jersey

Mainiero, J., Gillogly, B., Nease, O., Sherertz, D. and Wilkinson, P. (1971) *A Cross-Age Teaching Resource Manual*. Ontario-Montclair School District, Ontario, California. A highly practical guide for operating tutoring in primary schools. The headquarters of the School District are at 950 West D Street, Ontario, California 01764

Melaragno, R.J. (1976) *Tutoring with Students: a handbook for establishing tutoring programmes in schools*. Educational Technology Publications, Englewood Cliffs, New Jersey. The Tutorial Community Project of Melaragno and Newmark was based at 12961 Van Nuys Boulevard, Pacoima, California 91331

Niedermeyer, F.C. and Ellis, P.A. 'The SWRL Tutorial Programme'.

The Southwest Regional Laboratory for Educational Research and Development was the venue for the development of this tutorial programme, which included 9–10 year-olds tutoring 5-year-olds, and tutoring in English as a second language. SWRL may be found at 11300 La Cienega Boulevard, Inglewood, California 90304

'Pause, Prompt and Praise'. In New Zealand further information about this technique is available from Professor T. Glynn, Education Department, University of Otago, PO Box 56, Dunedin. In the United Kingdom, information is available from Kevin Wheldall and Frank Merrett at the Centre for Child Study, Department of Educational Psychology, University of Birmingham, PO Box 363, Birmingham. More work has been reported using this technique in a peer tutoring format in the United Kingdom than in New Zealand, where the emphasis has tended to be more on parent tuition. Both centres should be able to indicate availability of a self-instructional manual in the technique itself, and videotapes for training may be purchased.

'Paired Reading'. The Paired Reading Training Pack (second edition) (1986) includes written materials relevant to the planning, operating and evaluating of peer tutored Paired Reading projects, and a training video is also available. A separate video training pack has been produced to facilitate the training of spouses, friends, relatives and workmates as informal but regular and frequent tutors of Paired Reading for adults with literacy problems — the Ryedale Adult Literacy Training Pack. Both packs are distributed internationally from the Paired Reading Project, Directorate of Educational Services, Oldgate House, Huddersfield, HD1 6QW, West Yorkshire. Information about Cued Spelling is also available from this address.

Science Research Associates publish a number of kits of materials which lend themselves to interactive work in the peer tutoring situation. The SQ3R technique for developing reading comprehension is particularly associated with their series of 'Reading Laboratories'. SRA are located at Newtown Road, Henley-on-Thames, Oxfordshire RG9 1EW, United Kingdom, and 155 N. Wacker, Chicago, Illinois 60606, USA. The catalogues of other educational publishers are worth scrutinising carefully for materials and packages which might prove especially suitable for peer tutoring programmes — but don't forget to investigate materials already in school first.

Weinstein, G. (1970) *Youth Tutoring Youth: a manual for trainees*. This and other practical manuals and materials were available from the National Commission on Resources for Youth, 36 West 44th

Street, New York, 10036. (Some of them are also retrievable from ERIC under the reference ED 063543.)

FURTHER READING

Allen, V.L. (ed.) (1976) *Children as Teachers: theory and research on tutoring*. Academic Press, New York

Bloom, S. (ed.) (1975) *Peer and Cross-Age Tutoring in the Schools: an individualised supplement to group instruction*. US Department of Health, Education and Welfare, Washington, DC (ERIC ED 118543)

Ehly, S.W. and Larsen, S.C. (1980) *Peer Tutoring for Individualised Instruction*. Allyn and Bacon, Boston

Ellson, D.G. (1976) 'Tutoring' in N. Gage (ed.) *The Psychology of Teaching Methods*. University of Chicago Press, Chicago. (Includes discussion of tutoring by parents and para-professional adults.)

Fitz-Gibbon, C.T. (1977) *An Analysis of the Literature on Cross-Age Tutoring*. National Institute of Education, Washington, DC (ERIC ED 148807). Carol Fitz-Gibbon has also compiled a bibliography of items on peer tutoring available in the Brian Stanley Library at the University of Newcastle-upon-Tyne. This should be available from the School of Education, St Thomas Street, Newcastle-upon-Tyne, NE1 7RU

Gartner, A., Kohler, M. and Riessman, F. (1971) *Children Teach Children: learning by teaching*. Harper and Row, New York

Goodlad, S. (1979) *Learning by Teaching: an introduction to tutoring*. Community Service Volunteers, London. Available from C.S.V., 237 Pentonville Road, London, N1 9NJ. To order quote the ISBN number: ISBN 0 9501450 4 1

Klaus, D.G. (1975) *Patterns of Peer Tutoring*. American Institutes of Research, Washington, DC (ERIC ED 103356)

Paired Reading. A large number of peer tutor projects utilising the technique of Paired Reading are written up in the *Paired Reading Bulletin*. This is produced annually, and distributed internationally by the Paired Reading Project, Directorate of Educational Services, Oldgate House, Huddersfield, HD1 6QW, West Yorkshire

Rosenshine, B. and Furst, N. (1969) *The Effects of Tutoring upon Pupil Achievement: a research review*. Office of Education, Washington, DC (ERIC ED 064462)

Scruggs, T.E., Mastropieri, N.A. and Richter, L. (1985) 'Peer Tutoring with Behaviorally Disordered Students: social and academic benefits'. *Behavioral Disorders* 10, 4, 283–94

Stainback, W.C., Stainback, S.B. and Lichtward, F. (1975) 'The Research Evidence Regarding the Student to Student Tutoring Approach to Individualised Instruction'. *Educational Technology* 15, 54–6

Topping, K.J. and Wolfendale, S.W. (eds.) (1985) *Parental Involvement in Children's Reading.* Nichols, New York and Croom Helm, London

Wilkes, R. (1975) '*Peer and Cross-Age Tutoring and Related Topics: an annotated bibliography*'. (ERIC ED 115372)

HANDOUT FOR PARENTS

This specimen handout, designed to inform and reassure parents (or teachers!), may be photocopied for immediate use.

PEER TUTORING: A BRIEF GUIDE

Part of life at school asks children to try to do better than other children. But another very important part of school life is helping other people. Children learn well in both ways.

History

Peer tutoring means having children help other children to learn. Sometimes older children help younger children, and sometimes more able children help less able children of the same age. The idea is a very old one, first noted about 400 years ago. In Britain, Bell and Lancaster used peer tutoring a lot about 200 years ago. By 1816, 100,000 children were learning in this way. Peer tutoring then caught on in quite a few parts of the world.

As more and more schools for everyone were set up, paid for out of taxes, peer tutoring was used less and less. Helping children learn was taken over by paid adult teachers. However, in the 1960s it began to be used again, especially in the United States. Teachers came to grasp that peer tutoring was a great 'boost' or extra help for all children. Today, peer tutoring is again spreading rapidly in many parts of the world.

Effects

Many peer tutor projects work on reading, the most vital skill of all. But a wide range of other subjects have also been peer tutored, including mathematics, spelling, writing, languages and science. The tutors are not just being 'used', because they gain as much, if not more, than the tutees. To be able to tutor a subject, you have to really get to understand it well. So tutoring helps the *tutors* learn faster, too.

There is no doubt that peer tutoring 'works'. There is a lot of research to show that in peer tutor projects, the tutors improve in the tutored subject area as much, if not more than, the tutees, but at their own level. Many studies show that peer tutoring also improves how both tutor and tutee *feel* about the subject area — they get to like it more. Also, in many cases the tutor and tutee grow to like *each other* more, and get on better. There are many reports of both tutor and tutee showing more confidence and better behaviour. The research clearly shows that peer tutoring is one of the best ways of using school time.

Some projects have tutors and tutees of the same age, and some have older children as the tutors. Any difference in age does not seem to matter, as long as the tutor is more able in the subject area than the tutee. If the tutors and tutees are not too far apart in age and ability, there may be even more chance of the tutor gaining as a result. Some schools are now tutoring with pairs of the same ability, where the job of tutor switches from one to the other (this needs very careful planning).

Planning

Peer tutoring takes time and care to set up properly, and it is the paid teacher who has the skill to do this. Plans must be made about matching child pairs, finding the right sort of materials, training tutors and tutees, and lots of other points of organisation. However, this time is worthwhile, for peer tutoring is very effective. It is highly effective when you think of what is gained from a quite small amount of professional teacher time. For many pairs, peer tutoring has good spin-off in terms of better social harmony and more interest in other subject areas. Teachers often start peer tutoring in reading, but then become more confident in using the method in other subject areas.

Scope

Some primary (elementary) schools are now offering all young children the chance to be a tutee, and all the older children the chance to be a tutor. This helps to settle the young children into the school socially, and gives a boost to the older children, who feel very grown-up and responsible. In high schools parents can often lose touch with what their children are doing, but peer tutoring is often more and more popular with children as they move up through the school. Like any other way of effective teaching or managing learning, setting up peer tutor projects needs enthusiasm, careful planning and hard work on the part of the teacher. It would be a great mistake to think of peer tutoring as an easy option.

Further reading

Topping, K.J. (1987) *The Peer Tutoring Handbook: promoting co-operative learning*. Croom Helm, London

References

Albee, G.W. (1968) 'Conceptual models and manpower requirements in psychology'. *American Psychologist* 23, 317–20

Allen, V.L. (ed.) (1976) *Children as Teachers: theory and research on tutoring.* Academic Press, New York

Allen, V.L. and Devin-Sheehan, L.D. (1974) 'Cross-age interaction in one-teacher schools' in V.L. Allen (ed.) (1976) *Children as Teachers: theory and research on tutoring.* Academic Press, New York

Bar-Eli, N. and Raviv, A. (1982) 'Underachievers as tutors'. *Journal of Educational Research* 75, 3, 139–43

Bayliss, S. (1986) 'Yorkshire research shows 'pairing' lifts reading age'. *Times Educational Supplement* 7 March 1986, p. 8

Bell, A. (1797) *An Experiment in Education made at the Male Asylum of Madras: suggesting a system by which a school or family may teach itself under the superintendence of the master or parent.* Cadell & Davis, London

Bloom, B.S. (1984) 'The search for methods of group instruction as effective as one-to-one tutoring'. *Educational Leadership* 41, 8, 4–17

Bloom, S. (ed.) (1975) Peer and cross-age tutoring in the schools. US Department of Health, Education and Welfare, Washington, DC ERIC ED 118543

Branwhite, T. (1986) *Designing Special Programmes.* Methuen, London and New York

Briggs, D. (1974) 'Juniors in charge'. *Times Educational Supplement* 1 November 1974, p. 24

—— (1975) 'Across the ages'. *Times Educational Supplement* 15 August 1975, p. 9

Bronfenbrenner, U. (1970) *Two Worlds of Childhood.* Russell Sage Foundation, New York

Charconnet, M. (1975) 'Peer tutoring: operational description of various systems and their applications' in *Development of Educational Methods and Techniques Adapted to the Specific Conditions of the Developing Countries*, UNESCO, Paris

Cicirelli, V.G. (1976) 'Siblings teach siblings' in V.L. Allen (ed.) (1976) *Children as Teachers: theory and research on tutoring.* Academic Press, New York

Cohen, P.A., Kulik, J.A. and Kulik, C-L.C. (1982) 'Educational outcomes of tutoring: a meta-analysis of findings'. *American Educational Research Journal* 19, 2, 237–48

Custer, J.D. and Osguthorpe, R.T. (1983) 'Improving social acceptance by training handicapped students to tutor their non-handicapped peers'. *Exceptional Children* 50, 2, 173–5

Davies, L.L. and Layton, J.H. (1974) 'Peer and cross-age teaching: a warm fuzzy or a cold prickly' *Thrust for Educational Leadership* 3, 4, 20–1

Devin-Sheehan, L. *et al.* (1976) 'Research on children tutoring children: a critical review'. *Review of Educational Research* 46, 3, 355–85

Dickson, A. (1972) 'Each one, teach one'. *Frontier* June, 99–103

Doe, B. (1980) 'Children learn more by teaching their juniors'. *Times Educational Supplement* 4 March 1980, p. 21

Doyle, S. and Lobl, A. (1987) 'Embedding P.R. in the curriculum: parent tuition of top infants and cross-age peer tuition in the junior department'. *Paired Reading Bulletin* 3, 31–9

Eberwein, L. *et al.* (1976) 'An annotated bibliography on volunteer tutoring programs'. Paper presented at the south-east region reading conference of the International Reading Association (ERIC ED 117662)

Ehly, S.W. and Larsen, S.C. (1980) *Peer Tutoring for Individualized Instruction.* Allyn & Bacon, Boston

Ellson, D.G., Harris, P. and Barber, L. (1968) 'A field test of programed and directed tutoring'. *Reading Research Quarterly* 3, 307–67

Feldman, R.S., Devin-Sheehan, L. and Allen, V.L. (1976) 'Children tutoring children: a critical review of research' in V.L. Allen (ed.) (1976) *Children as Teachers: theory and research on tutoring.* Academic Press, New York

Fitz-Gibbon, C.T. and Reay, D.G. (1982) 'Peer tutoring: brightening up F.L. teaching in an urban comprehensive school'. *British Journal of Language Teaching* 20, 1, 39–44

Fletcher, R.K. and Fawcett, S.B. (1978) 'An open-learning centre for low-income adults'. *Educational Technology* 18, 55–9

Formentin, P. and Csapo, M. (1980) *Precision Teaching.* Centre for Human Resources and Development, Vancouver

Fowler, S.A., Dougherty, B.S., Kirby, K.C. and Kohler, F.W. (1986) 'Role reversals: an analysis of therapeutic effects achieved with disruptive boys during their appointments as peer monitors'. *Journal of Applied Behavior Analysis* 19, 4, 437–44

Gartner, S., Kohler, M. and Riessman, F. (1971) *Children Teach*

Children: learning by teaching. Harper & Row, New York

Gerber, M. and Kauffman, J.M. (1981) 'Peer tutoring in academic settings' in P.S. Strain (ed.) *The Utilization of Classroom Peers as Behavior Change Agents.* Plenum Press, New York and London

Glynn, T. (1985) 'Contexts for independent learning'. *Educational Psychology* 5, 1, 5–15

Goldstein, H. and Wickstrom, S. (1986) 'Peer intervention effects on communicative interaction among handicapped and nonhandicapped preschoolers'. *Journal of Applied Behavior Analysis* 19, 2, 209–14

Goodlad, S. (1979) *Learning by Teaching: an introduction to tutoring.* Community Service Volunteers, London

—— (1985) 'Putting science into context'. *Educational Research* 27, 1, 61–7

Gredler, G.R. (1985) 'An assessment of cross-age tutoring' *Techniques* 1, 3, 226–32

Harrison, G. von (1976) 'Structured tutoring: antidote for low achievement' in V.L. Allen (ed.) (1976) *Children as Teachers: theory and research on tutoring.* Academic Press, New York

Harrison, G. von and Reay, D.G. (1983) 'Tutoring in primary schools in the U.S.A.'. *Research in Education* 30, 65–9

Johnson, R.T. and Johnson, D.W. (1983) 'Effects of co-operative, competitive, and individualistic learning experiences on social development'. *Exceptional Children* 49, 4, 323–9

Karegianes, M.L., Pascarella, E.T. and Pflaum, S.W. (1980) 'The effects of peer editing on the writing proficiency of low-achieving 10th grade students'. *Journal of Educational Research* 73, 4, 203–7

Klaus, D.J. (1975) *'Patterns of Peer Tutoring'.* American Institutes of Research, Washington, DC (ERIC ED 103356)

Lancaster, J. (1803) *Improvements in education as it respects the industrious classes of the community, containing, among other important particulars, an account of the institution for the education of one thousand poor children, Borough Road, Southwark; and of the new system of education on which it is conducted.* Darton & Harvey, London

Lancioni, G.E. (1982) 'Normal children as tutors to teach social responses to withdrawn mentally retarded school mates: maintenance and generalization'. *Journal of Applied Behavior Analysis* 15, 17–40

Lawrence, D. (1972) 'Counselling of retarded readers by non-professionals'. *Educational Research* 15, 48–51

Lee, A. (1986) 'Sustained gains'. *Times Educational Supplement* 21 March 1986, p. 40

Limbrick, E., McNaughton, S. and Glynn, T. (1985) 'Reading gains for underachieving tutors and tutees in a cross-age tutoring programme'. *Journal of Child Psychology and Psychiatry* 26, 6, 939–53

Lobato, D. (1985) 'Preschool siblings of handicapped children: impact of peer support and training'. *Journal of Autism and Developmental Disorders* 15, 3, 345–50

Maher, C.A. (1982) 'Behavioral effects of using conduct problem adolescents as cross-age tutors'. *Psychology in the Schools* 19, 360–64

—— (1984) 'Handicapped adolescents as cross-age tutors: program description and evaluation'. *Exceptional Children* 51, 1, 56–63

Melaragno, R.J. (1974) 'Beyond decoding: systematic schoolwide tutoring in reading'. *The Reading Teacher* 27, 157–60

Murfitt, J. and Thomas, J.B. (1983) 'The effects of peer counselling on the self-concept and reading attainment of secondary aged slow learning pupils'. *Remedial Education* 18, 2, 73–4

Palincsar, A.S. and Brown, A.L. (1986) 'Interactive teaching to promote independent learning from text'. *The Reading Teacher* 39, 8, 771–7

Pigott, H.E., Fantuzzo, J.W. and Clement, P.W. (1986) 'The effects of reciprocal peer tutoring and group contingencies on the academic performance of elementary school children'. *Journal of Applied Behavior Analaysis* 19, 1, 93–8

Posen, B. (1983) '*Peer Tutoring among Young Offenders: two experiments'. Unpublished M.Ed. thesis, University of Newcastle-upon-Tyne*

Reigert, J.F. (1916) *The Lancasterian System of Instruction in the Schools of New York City.* Arno Press, New York. (Republished 1969.)

Roper, R.J. (1975) 'Mutual advantage when VIth form help teach lower school'. *Times Educational Supplement* 21 March 1975, p. 32

Rosenbaum, P.S. (1973) *Peer-mediated Instruction.* Teachers' College Press, New York

Russell, T. and Ford, D.F. (1983) 'Effectiveness of peer tutors vs. resource teachers'. *Psychology in the Schools* 20, 436–41

Sainato, D.M., Maheady, L. and Shook, G.L. (1986) 'The effects of a classroom manager role on the social interaction patterns and social status of withdrawn kindergarten students'. *Journal of Applied Behavior Analysis* 19, 2, 187–95

Scoble, J., Topping, K.J. and Wigglesworth, C. (1987) 'Training family and friends as adult literacy tutors'. *Journal of Reading* (in press)

Scruggs, T.E., Mastropieri, M.A. and Richter, L. (1985) 'Peer tutoring with behaviorally disordered students: social and academic benefits'. *Behavioral Disorders* 10, 4, 283–94

Scruggs, T.E. and Osguthorpe, R.T. (1986) 'Tutoring interventions within special education settings: a comparison of cross-age and peer tutoring'. *Psychology in the Schools* 23, 2, 187–93

Sharan, S. (1980) 'Cooperative learning in small groups: recent methods and effects on achievement, attitudes and ethnic relations'. *Review of Educational Research* 50, 241–71

Sharpley, A.M. and Sharpley, C.F. (1981) 'Peer tutoring: a review of the literature'. *Collected Original Resources in Education* (CORE) 5, 3, 7–C11 (fiche 7 and 8). (CORE is produced by Carfax Publishing Company, PO Box 125, Abingdon, Oxfordshire, OX14 3UE. In the United States: 35 South Street, Hopkinton, Ma. 01748)

Sindelar, P.T. (1982) 'The effects of cross-aged tutoring on the comprehension skills of remedial reading students'. *The Journal of Special Education* 16, 2, 199–206

Stott, D.H. (1974) *The Social Adjustment of Children* (5th edition). Hodder & Stoughton, London

Stowitschek, C., Hecimovic, A., Stowitschek, J. and Shores, R. (1982) 'Behaviorally disordered adolescents as peer tutors: immediate and generative effects on instructional performance and spelling achievement'. *Behavioral Disorders* 7, 136–48

Strain, P.S. (ed.) (1981) *The Utilization of Classroom Peers as Behavior Change Agents*. Plenum Press, New York

Topping, K.J. (1983) *Educational Systems for Disruptive Adolescents*. St Martin's Press, New York and Croom Helm, London

—— (1986) *The Kirklees Paired Reading Training Pack* (second edition). Kirklees Directorate of Educational Services, Huddersfield, England

—— (1987a) 'Reading Together: how to organise peer tutoring'. *Junior Education* 11, 3, 28–9

—— (1987b) 'Peer tutored Paired Reading: outcome data from ten projects'. *Educational Psychology* 7, 2, 133–45

Topping, K.J. and Wolfendale, S.W. (eds.) (1985) *Parental Involvement in Children's Reading*. Nichols, New York and Croom Helm, London

Townsend, J. and Topping, K.J. (1986) 'An experiment using Paired Reading with peer tutors vs. parent tutors at High Bank First

School'. *Paired Reading Bulletin 2, 26–31.*

Trovato, J. and Bucher, B. (1980) 'Peer tutoring with or without home-based reinforcement, for reading remediation'. *Journal of Applied Behavior Analysis* 13, 1, 129–41

Warner, R. and Scott, S. (1974) 'Peer counselling'. *Personnel and Guidance Journal* 53, 228–31

Wheldall, K. and Mettem, P. (1985) 'Behavioural peer tutoring: training 16-year-old tutors to employ the "Pause, Prompt and Praise" method with 12-year-old remedial readers'. *Educational Psychology* 5, 1, 27–44

Wilkes, R. (1975) *'Peer and Cross-Age Tutoring and Related Topics: an annotated bibliography'.* (ERIC ED 115372)

Winter, S. (1986) 'Peers as Paired Reading tutors'. *British Journal of Special Education* 13, 3, 103–6

Winter, S. and Low, A. (1984) 'The Rossmere Peer Tutor Project'. *Behavioural Approaches with Children* 8, 2, 62–5